OpenStack for Architects

Design and implement successful private clouds with
OpenStack

Michael Solberg
Ben Silverman

BIRMINGHAM - MUMBAI

OpenStack for Architects

First published: January 2017

Production reference: 1310117

Published by Packt Publishing Ltd.
Livery Place
35 Livery Street
Birmingham
B3 2PB, UK.
ISBN 978-1-78439-510-0

www.packtpub.com

Credits

Authors
Michael Solberg
Ben Silverman

Reviewer
Lauren Malhoit

Commissioning Editor
Veena Pagare

Acquisition Editor
Meeta Rajani

Content Development Editors
Radhika Atitkar
Sanjeet Rao

Technical Editor
Nidhisha Shetty

Copy Editor
Tom Jacob

Project Coordinator
Judie Jose

Proofreader
Safis Editing

Indexer
Francy Puthiry

Graphics
Kirk D'Penha

Production Coordinator
Shantanu Zagade

About the Authors

Michael Solberg, as a chief architect, is responsible for helping Red Hat customers achieve their key business transformation initiatives through open source architectures and technologies. He regularly advises a range of Fortune 100 companies in financial services, healthcare, retail, and transportation verticals on topics such as cloud computing, big data, high-performance computing, and enterprise middleware. At Red Hat since 2008, Michael has led a number of successful initiatives to assist strategic customers adopt new virtualization, systems management, and engineering practices. His previous experience includes building web hosting infrastructure. He is also an avid supporter of the OpenStack project. Michael holds a Bachelor's degree from the University of Georgia and is a regular speaker at industry events.

I would like to thank Kyle Gonzales and Brent Holden for their early work on the project. Huge thanks to Joseph Scalia for reviewing the book and continually encouraging me to work on the project.

Ben Silverman, as the Principal Cloud Architect for OnX Enterprise Solutions, is responsible for providing strategic and tactical cloud leadership to OnX's customers. Previously, Ben was a Senior Cloud Architect at Mirantis, where he developed cloud solutions for many Fortune 100 companies. Ben has been involved with OpenStack since the Havana release and is an active technical contributor. Prior to working for Mirantis, Ben was the Lead Technical Architect at American Express, where he built one of the largest financial services OpenStack clouds at that time. Ben is an exuberant OpenStack evangelist who is often seen speaking at industry events and conventions about OpenStack adoption, scale challenges, and cloud operations. In his limited spare time, Ben and a few others have taken on the task of re-writing all of the OpenStack architecture and operations guides that are currently available on the OpenStack Foundation website. Ben has a Master's degree in Information Management from Arizona State University and lives in Phoenix, AZ.

I would like to thank my wife, Jennifer, and my two sons, Jason and Brayden, for all of the love and encouragement, as well as the necessary interruptions to make me smile with a hug, a kiss, a silly comment, or a new drawing for daddy's desk.

www.PacktPub.com

For support files and downloads related to your book, please visit www.PacktPub.com.

Did you know that Packt offers eBook versions of every book published, with PDF and ePub files available? You can upgrade to the eBook version at www.PacktPub.com and as a print book customer, you are entitled to a discount on the eBook copy. Get in touch with us at service@packtpub.com for more details.

At www.PacktPub.com, you can also read a collection of free technical articles, sign up for a range of free newsletters and receive exclusive discounts and offers on Packt books and eBooks.

https://www.packtpub.com/mapt

Get the most in-demand software skills with Mapt. Mapt gives you full access to all Packt books and video courses, as well as industry-leading tools to help you plan your personal development and advance your career.

Why subscribe?

- Fully searchable across every book published by Packt
- Copy and paste, print, and bookmark content
- On demand and accessible via a web browser

Customer Feedback

Thank you for purchasing this Packt book. We take our commitment to improving our content and products to meet your needs seriously—that's why your feedback is so valuable. Whatever your feelings about your purchase, please consider leaving a review on this book's Amazon page. Not only will this help us, more importantly it will also help others in the community to make an informed decision about the resources that they invest in to learn. You can also review for us on a regular basis by joining our reviewers' club. **If you're interested in joining, or would like to learn more about the benefits we offer, please contact us**: customerreviews@packtpub.com.

Table of Contents

Preface

This guide leads you through each of the major decision points that you'll face as you architect an OpenStack private cloud for your organization. At each point, we offer you advice based on years of experience designing and leading successful OpenStack projects in a wide range of industries. Each chapter also includes lab materials that give you a chance to install and configure the technologies used to build production-quality OpenStack clouds. Most importantly, we focus on ensuring that your OpenStack project meets the needs of your organization, which will guarantee a successful roll-out.

What this book covers

Chapter 1, *Introducing OpenStack*, helps you familiarize yourself with the components of OpenStack.

Chapter 2, *Architecting the Cloud*, explains the software, hardware, network, and storage selection options for OpenStack.

Chapter 3, *Planning for Failure (and Success)*, covers techniques of increasing the scalability and availability of the cloud.

Chapter 4, *Building the Deployment Pipeline*, shows how to use the concepts of DevOps to create a continuously integrated and delivered OpenStack deployment.

Chapter 5, *Building to Operate*, explains how to architect a private cloud that is optimized for operations.

Chapter 6, *Integrating the Platform*, reveals three different integration patterns for OpenStack clouds.

Chapter 7, *Securing the Cloud*, introduces how to design a private cloud that is secure from the beginning.

Chapter 8, *Conclusion*, covers creating a compelling road map for the future of Infrastructure as a Service in your organization.

What you need for this book

All of the software used in the examples in this book is available at no cost on the Internet. Links are provided for each of the projects used. Many of the lab exercises require access to physical hardware. We recommend having at least four and up to 12 physical servers available for deploying OpenStack.

Who this book is for

This book is written especially for those who will design OpenStack clouds and lead their implementation. These people are typically cloud architects, but may also be in product management, systems engineering, or enterprise architecture.

Conventions

In this book, you will find a number of text styles that distinguish between different kinds of information. Here are some examples of these styles and an explanation of their meaning.

Code words in text, database table names, folder names, filenames, file extensions, pathnames, dummy URLs, user input, and Twitter handles are shown as follows: "The keystonerc_admin file can be used to authenticate an administrative user and the keystonerc_demo file can be used to authenticate a non-privileged user."

A block of code is set as follows:

```
export OS_USERNAME=demo
export OS_TENANT_NAME=demo
export OS_PASSWORD=<random string>
export OS_AUTH_URL=http://192.168.0.10:5000/v2.0/
export PS1='[\u@\h \W(keystone_demo)]\$ '
```

When we wish to draw your attention to a particular part of a code block, the relevant lines or items are set in bold:

```
export OS_USERNAME=demo
export OS_TENANT_NAME=demo
export OS_PASSWORD=<random string>
export OS_AUTH_URL=http://192.168.0.10:5000/v2.0/
export PS1='[\u@\h \W(keystone_demo)]\$ '
```

Any command-line input or output is written as follows:

```
# yum install -y openstack-packstack
```

New terms and **important words** are shown in bold. Words that you see on the screen, for example, in menus or dialog boxes, appear in the text like this: "Click on the **Manage Jenkins** link in the left-hand navigation."

Warnings or important notes appear in a box like this.

Tips and tricks appear like this.

Reader feedback

Feedback from our readers is always welcome. Let us know what you think about this book-what you liked or disliked. Reader feedback is important for us as it helps us develop titles that you will really get the most out of. To send us general feedback, simply e-mail feedback@packtpub.com, and mention the book's title in the subject of your message. If there is a topic that you have expertise in and you are interested in either writing or contributing to a book, see our author guide at www.packtpub.com/authors.

Customer support

Now that you are the proud owner of a Packt book, we have a number of things to help you to get the most from your purchase.

Downloading the example code

You can download the example code files for this book from your account at http://www.packtpub.com. If you purchased this book elsewhere, you can visit http://www.packtpub.com/support and register to have the files e-mailed directly to you.

You can download the code files by following these steps:

1. Log in or register to our website using your e-mail address and password.
2. Hover the mouse pointer on the **SUPPORT** tab at the top.
3. Click on **Code Downloads & Errata**.
4. Enter the name of the book in the **Search** box.
5. Select the book for which you're looking to download the code files.
6. Choose from the drop-down menu where you purchased this book from.
7. Click on **Code Download**.

Once the file is downloaded, please make sure that you unzip or extract the folder using the latest version of:

- WinRAR / 7-Zip for Windows
- Zipeg / iZip / UnRarX for Mac
- 7-Zip / PeaZip for Linux

The code bundle for the book is also hosted on GitHub at `https://github.com/PacktPublishing/OpenStack-for-Architects`. We also have other code bundles from our rich catalog of books and videos available at `https://github.com/PacktPublishing/`. Check them out!

Downloading the color images of this book

We also provide you with a PDF file that has color images of the screenshots/diagrams used in this book. The color images will help you better understand the changes in the output. You can download this file from `https://www.packtpub.com/sites/default/files/downloads/OpenStackforArchitects_ColorImages.pdf`.

Errata

Although we have taken every care to ensure the accuracy of our content, mistakes do happen. If you find a mistake in one of our books-maybe a mistake in the text or the code-we would be grateful if you could report this to us. By doing so, you can save other readers from frustration and help us improve subsequent versions of this book. If you find any errata, please report them by visiting http://www.packtpub.com/submit-errata, selecting your book, clicking on the **Errata Submission Form** link, and entering the details of your errata. Once your errata are verified, your submission will be accepted and the errata will be uploaded to our website or added to any list of existing errata under the Errata section of that title.

To view the previously submitted errata, go to https://www.packtpub.com/books/content/support and enter the name of the book in the search field. The required information will appear under the **Errata** section.

Piracy

Piracy of copyrighted material on the Internet is an ongoing problem across all media. At Packt, we take the protection of our copyright and licenses very seriously. If you come across any illegal copies of our works in any form on the Internet, please provide us with the location address or website name immediately so that we can pursue a remedy.

Please contact us at copyright@packtpub.com with a link to the suspected pirated material.

We appreciate your help in protecting our authors and our ability to bring you valuable content.

Questions

If you have a problem with any aspect of this book, you can contact us at questions@packtpub.com, and we will do our best to address the problem.

1
Introducing OpenStack

At the Vancouver OpenStack Conference in May 2015, US retail giant Walmart announced that they had deployed an OpenStack cloud with 140,000 cores of compute supporting 1.5 billion page views on Cyber Monday. CERN, a long-time OpenStack user, announced that their OpenStack private cloud had grown to 100,000 cores running computational workloads on two petabytes of disk in production. Another 250 companies and organizations across nine industry verticals have announced that they have adopted OpenStack in their data centers.

OpenStack had completely redrawn the private cloud landscape in the five short years of its existence. In this chapter, we'll look at what OpenStack is and why it has been so influential. We'll also take the first steps in architecting a cloud.

What is OpenStack?

OpenStack is best defined by its use cases, as users and contributors approach the software with many different goals in mind. For hosting providers such as Rackspace, OpenStack provides the infrastructure for a multitenant shared services platform. For others, it might provide a mechanism for provisioning data and compute for a distributed business intelligence application. There are a few answers to this question that are relevant regardless of your organization's use case.

OpenStack is an API

One of the initial goals of OpenStack was to provide **Application Program Interface (API)** compatibility with the Amazon Web Service. As of the November 2014 user survey, 44% of production deployments were still using the EC2 Compatibility API to interact with the system. As the popularity of the platform has increased, the OpenStack API has become a de facto standard on its own. As such, many of the enterprise organizations that we've worked with to create OpenStack clouds are using them as an underlying Infrastructure as a Service layer for one or more Platform as a Service or Hybrid Cloud deployments.

Every feature or function of OpenStack is exposed in one of its REST APIs. There are command-line interfaces for OpenStack (legacy `nova` and the newer `openstack common client`) as well as a standard web interface (Horizon). However, most interactions between the components and end users happen over the API. This is advantageous for the following reasons:

- Everything in the system can be automated
- Integration with other systems is well defined
- Use cases can be clearly defined and automatically tested

The APIs are well defined and versioned REST APIs, and there are native clients and SDKs for more than a dozen programming languages. For a full list of current SDKs, refer to `http://api.openstack.org`.

OpenStack – an open source software project

OpenStack is an open source software project which has a huge number of contributors from a wide range of organizations. OpenStack was originally created by NASA and Rackspace. Rackspace is still a significant contributor to OpenStack, but these days contributions to the project come from a wide array of companies, including the traditional open source contributors (Red Hat, IBM, and HP) as well as companies which are dedicated entirely to OpenStack (Mirantis, and CloudBase). Contributions come in the form of drivers for particular pieces of infrastructure (that is, Cinder block storage drivers or Neutron SDN drivers), bug fixes, or new features in the core projects.

OpenStack is governed by a foundation. Membership in the foundation is free and open to anyone who wishes to join. There are currently thousands of members in the foundation. Leadership on technical issues is provided by a thirteen-member technical committee, which is generally elected by the individual members. Strategic and financial issues are decided by a board of directors, which includes members appointed by corporate sponsors and elected by the individual members.

 For more information on joining or contributing to the OpenStack Foundation, refer to `http://www.openstack.org/foundation`.

OpenStack is written in the Python programming language and is usually deployed on the Linux operating system. The source code is readily available on the Internet and commits are welcome from the community at large. Before code is committed to the project, it has to pass through a series of gates, which include unit testing and code review.

 For more information on committing code to OpenStack, refer to `https://wiki.openstack.org/wiki/How_To_Contribute`.

OpenStack – a private cloud platform

Finally, OpenStack provides the software modules necessary to build an automated private cloud platform. While OpenStack has traditionally been focused on providing Infrastructure as a Service capabilities in the style of Amazon Web Services, new projects have been introduced lately, which begin to provide capabilities which might be associated more with Platform as a Service. This book will focus on implementing the core set of OpenStack components described as follows.

The most important aspect of OpenStack pertaining to its usage as a private cloud platform is the tenant model. The authentication and authorization services which provide this model are implemented in the Identity service, Keystone. Every virtual or physical object governed by the OpenStack system exists within a private space referred to as a **tenant** or **project**. The latest version of the Keystone API has differentiated itself further to include a higher level construct called a **domain**. Regardless of the terminology, the innate ability to securely segregate compute, network, and storage resources is the most fundamental capability of the platform. This is what differentiates it from traditional data center virtualization and makes it a private cloud platform.

OpenStack components

OpenStack is a modular system. While some OpenStack Architects choose to implement a reference architecture of all of the core components shipped by an OpenStack distributor, many will only implement the services required to meet their business cases.

Reference implementations are typically used for development use cases where the final production state of the service might not be well-defined. Production deployments will likely gate the availability of some services to reduce the amount of configuration and testing required for implementation. Reference deployments will typically not vary from the distributor's implementation, so that the distributor's deployment and testing tools can be reused without modification.

In this book, we'll be focusing on the following core components of OpenStack.

Compute

OpenStack Compute (Nova) is one of the original components of OpenStack. It provides the ability to provision a virtual machine, an application container, or a physical system, depending on configuration. All provisioning is image-based and the OpenStack Image Service (Glance) is a prerequisite for the Compute service. Some kind of networking is also required to launch a compute instance.

Networking was originally provided by the Compute service in OpenStack and some large deployments still use the networking functionality provided by the Nova service. Most modern deployments use the Neutron service. We'll discuss reasons why an architect might choose the Nova network service instead of the Neutron service in a later chapter.

In OpenStack, we refer to provisioned compute nodes as **instances** and not **virtual machines**. While this might seem like a matter of semantics, it's a useful device for a few reasons. The first reason is that it describes the deployment mechanism-all compute in OpenStack is the **instantiation** of a Glance image with a specified hardware template, the **flavor**.

The flavor describes the characteristics of the instantiated image-it normally represents a number of cores of compute with a given amount of memory and storage. Storage may be provided by the Compute service or may be provided by the block storage service, Cinder. While quotas are defined to limit the amount of cores, memory, and storage available to a given user (the tenant), charge-back is traditionally established by the flavor (that is, instantiating a particular image on an `m1-small` flavor may cost a tenant a certain number of cents an hour).

The second reason that the term instance is useful is that virtual machines in OpenStack do not typically have the same life cycle as they do in traditional virtualization. While we might expect virtual machines to have a multiyear life cycle like physical machines, we would expect instances to have a life cycle measured in days or weeks. Virtual machines are backed up and recovered, whereas instances are rescued or evacuated. A resize operation on a virtual machine might happen without downtime, while a resize operation on a instance is a new deployment and a migration. This is due to the architectural differences between OpenStack and traditional virtual machines and their hypervisors. Legacy virtualization platforms assume resizing and modifying behaviors in-place, cloud platforms such as OpenStack expect redeployment of virtual machines or adding additional capacity through additional instances, not adding additional resources to existing virtual machines. Even the term **migration** has a different meaning for an instance than we would expect for a virtual machine.

The third reason that we find it useful to use the term instance is that the Compute service has evolved over the years to launch a number of different types of compute. Some OpenStack deployments may only launch physical machines, whereas others may launch a combination of physical, virtual, and container-based instances. The same construct applies regardless of the compute provider.

Some of the lines between virtual machines and instances are becoming more blurred as more enterprise features are added to the OpenStack Compute service. Later on, we'll discuss some of the ways in which we can launch instances which act more like virtual machines for more traditional compute workloads.

Object Storage

Ephemeral backing storage for compute instances is provided by the Nova service. This storage is referred to as **ephemeral** because its life cycle coterminates with the life cycle of the compute instance. That is, when an instance is terminated, the ephemeral storage associated with the instance is deleted from the compute host on which it resided. The first kind of persistent storage provided in the OpenStack system was object storage, based on the S3 service available in the Amazon Web Service environment.

Object Storage is provided by the Swift service in OpenStack. Just as Nova provides an EC2-compatible compute API, Swift provides an S3-compatible object storage API. Applications which are written to run on the Amazon EC2 service and read and write their persistent data to the S3 Object Storage service do not need to be rewritten to run on an OpenStack system.

A number of third-party applications provide an S3 or Swift-compatible API and may be substituted for Swift in a typical OpenStack deployment. These include open source object stores such as Gluster or Ceph or proprietary ones such as Scality or Riak. The Swift service is broken down into a few components and third-party applications may use the "Proxy" component of Swift for API services and implement only a backend or may entirely replace the Swift service. All OpenStack-compatible object stores will consume the tenant model of OpenStack and accept Keystone tokens for authentication.

Block storage

Traditional persistent storage is provided to OpenStack workloads via the Cinder block storage component. The life cycle of Cinder volumes is maintained independent of compute instances, and volumes may be attached or detached to one or more compute instances to provide a backing store for filesystem-based storage.

OpenStack ships with a reference implementation of Cinder, which leverages local storage on the host and utilizes LVM as well as the ability to use iSCSI to share a block device attached to a Cinder **storage node** that can use its storage for instances. This implementation lacks high availability and is typically only used in test environments. Production deployments tend to leverage a software-based or hardware-based block storage solution such as Ceph or NetApp, chosen based on performance and availability requirements.

Network

The last of the foundational services in OpenStack is Neutron, the Network service. Neutron provides an API for creating ports, subnets, networks, and routers. Additional network services such as firewalls and load balancers are provided in some OpenStack deployments.

As with Cinder, the reference implementation, based on Open vSwitch, is typically used in test environments or smaller deployments. Large-scale production deployments will leverage one of the many available software-based or hardware-based SDN solutions which have Neutron drivers. These solutions range from open source implementations such as Juniper's OpenContrail and Midokura's MidoNet to proprietary solutions such as VMware's NSX platform.

As mentioned earlier, there are still some OpenStack Architects who chose to deploy clouds based on the Network service included with Nova instead of the neutron component. This decision is largely made based on the lack of distributed routing capabilities in the Neutron reference plugin. In the current reference implementation, Neutron simply uses a centralized node for routing with a passive node as its highly available failover. Newer versions of OpenStack are now supporting a **Distributed Virtual Router** (**DVR**) reference implementation, however, additional performance testing is required in order to ascertain whether this model provides significant performance increases. However, as the Nova network implementation has become deprecated and additional capabilities have matured within the Neutron reference implementation, more and more deployments are using Neutron.

Common OpenStack use cases

In spite of immense interest, huge investment, and public success, we've seen a number of cases where well-intentioned OpenStack projects fail or are at least perceived as a failure by the people who have funded them. When OpenStack projects fail, the technology itself is rarely the root cause. Thomas Bittman at Gartner noticed this trend and wrote an influential blog post entitled *Why are Private Clouds Failing?* in September 2014.

Bittman's findings echo many of our experiences from the field. In short, the reason that most private cloud projects fail is that improper expectations were set from the beginning and the business goals for the cloud weren't realized by the end result.

First and foremost, OpenStack deployments should be seen as an investment with returns and not a project to reduce operational costs. While we've certainly seen dramatic reductions in operational workloads through the automation that OpenStack provides, it is difficult to accurately quantify those reductions in order to justify the operational investment required to run an efficient cloud platform. Organizations that are entirely focused on cutting costs through automation should first look at automating existing virtual environments instead of deploying new environments.

We've also seen a lot of projects which had poorly quantified goals. OpenStack is an enabler of use cases and not an IT panacea. If the use cases are not agreed upon before investment in the platform begins, it will prove very difficult to justify the investment in the end. This is why the role of the Architect is so critical in OpenStack deployments-it is their job to ensure that concrete requirements are written upfront so that all of the stakeholders can quantify the success of the platform once deployed.

With that in mind, let's take a look at some typical use cases for OpenStack deployments.

Public hosting

As we mentioned before, OpenStack was originally created with code contributions from NASA and Rackspace. NASA's interest in OpenStack sprang from their desire to create a private elastic compute cloud while the primary goal for Rackspace was to create an open source platform that could replace their public shared hosting infrastructure. As of April 2015, the "Rackspace Public Cloud" offering had been ported to OpenStack and had passed the **OpenStack Powered Platform** certification.

The Rackspace implementation offers both Compute and Object Storage services, but some implementations may choose to offer only Compute or Object Storage and receive certifications for those services. DreamHost, another public OpenStack-based cloud provider, for example, has chosen to break their managed services down into **DreamCompute** and **DreamObjects**, which implement the services separately. The DreamObjects service was implemented and offered first as a compliment to DreamHost's existing shared web hosting and the DreamCompute service was introduced later.

Most public hosting providers focus primarily on the Compute service and many do not yet offer software-defined networking via the Neutron network service (DreamCompute being a notable exception). Architects of hosting platforms will focus first on tenancy issues, secondly on chargeback issues, and lastly on scale. We've seen some amazing work done around instrumentation and monitoring of public clouds as well; refer to Rackspace's work around StackTach for more information on that at the following URL:
`https://media.readthedocs.org/pdf/stacktach/latest/stacktach.pdf`

High-performance compute

The first production deployment of OpenStack outside NASA and Rackspace was at a Canadian not-for-profit organization named Cybera. Cybera deployed OpenStack as a technology platform in 2011 for its DAIR program, which provides free compute and storage to Canadian researchers, entrepreneurs, and small businesses.

Architects at Cybera, NASA, and CERN have all commented on how their services have much of the same concerns as in the public hosting space. They provide compute and storage resources to researchers and don't have much insight into how those resources will actually be used. Thus, concerns about secure multitenancy will apply to these environments just as much as they do in the hosting space.

HPC clouds will have an added focus on performance, though. While hosting providers will look to economize on commodity hardware, research clouds will look to maximize performance by configuring their compute, storage, and network hardware to support high volume and throughput operations. Where most clouds will work best by growing low-to-mid range hardware horizontally with commodity hardware, high-performance clouds tend to be very specific about the performance profiles of their hardware selection. Cybera has published performance benchmarks comparing its DAIR platform to EC2. Architects of research clouds may also look to use hardware pass-through capabilities or other low-level hypervisor features to enable specific workloads.

Rapid application development

Over the last couple of years, a third significant use case has emerged for OpenStack-enterprise application development environments. While public hosting and high-performance Compute implementations may have huge regions with hundreds of compute nodes and thousands of cores, enterprise implementations tend to have regions of 20 to 50 compute nodes. Enterprise adopters have a strong interest in software-defined networking.

The primary driver for enterprise adoption of OpenStack has been the increasing use of continuous integration and continuous delivery in the application development workflow. A typical **Continuous Integration and Continuous Delivery (CI/CD)** workflow will deploy a complete application on every developer commit which passes basic unit tests in order to perform automated integration testing. These application deployments live as long as it takes to run the unit tests and then an automated process tears down the deployment once the tests pass or fail. This workflow is easily facilitated with a combination of OpenStack Compute and Network services. Indeed, 92% of OpenStack users reported using their private clouds for CI/CD workflows in the Kilo user survey.

While Architects of hosting or **High-performance Computing** (**HPC**) clouds spend a lot of time focusing on tenancy and scale issues, Architects of enterprise deployments will spend a lot of time focusing on how to integrate OpenStack compute into their existing infrastructure. Enterprise deployments will frequently leverage existing service catalog implementations and identity management solutions. Many enterprise deployments will also need to integrate with existing IPAM and asset tracking systems.

Network Function Virtualization

An emerging and exciting use case for OpenStack is **Network Function Virtualization** (**NFV**). NFV solves a problem particular to the telecommunications industry, which is in the process of replacing the purpose-built hardware devices which provide network services with virtualized appliances which run on commodity hardware. Some of these services are routing, proxies, content filtering as well as packet core services and high-volume switching. Most of these appliances have intense compute requirements and are largely stateless. These workloads are well-suited for the OpenStack compute model.

NFV use cases typically leverage hardware features which can directly attach compute instances to physical network interfaces on compute nodes. Instances are also typically very sensitive to CPU and memory topology (NUMA) and virtual cores tend to be mapped directly to physical cores. These deployments focus heavily on the Compute service and typically don't make use of OpenStack services such as Object Storage or Orchestration.

Architects of NFV solutions will focus primarily on virtual instance placement and performance issues and less on tenancy and integration issues.

Drafting an initial deployment plan

OpenStack is designed to be used at scale. Many IT projects might comprise a few physical assets deployed within an existing network, storage, and compute landscape, but OpenStack deployments are, by definition, new network, storage, and compute landscapes. Any project of this size and scope requires significant coordination between different teams within an IT organization. This kind of coordination requires careful planning and, in our experience, a lot of documentation.

The role of the Architect

This book is written to provide best practices for a relatively new role within many organizations-the Cloud Architect. The Cloud Architect's primary function is to take business requirements for Infrastructure or Platform as a Service and design an Infrastructure or Platform as a Service solution which meets those requirements. This requires an in-depth knowledge of the capabilities of the infrastructure software paired with competency in network and storage architecture.

The typical Cloud Architect will have a background in compute and will lean heavily on the Network and Storage Architects within an organization to round out their technical knowledge. Since OpenStack is based on the Linux operating system, most OpenStack Architects will have a deep knowledge of that platform. But as we mentioned earlier, OpenStack is typically delivered as an API and OpenStack Architects will need to have fluency in application development as well.

OpenStack Architects are responsible first and foremost for authoring and maintaining a set of design and deployment documentation. It's difficult to describe an ocean if you've never seen one, so this book will walk you through implementation of the documentation that you will create as you create it.

The design document

The first document that we will create is the design document. This may be called something different in your organization, but the goal of the design document is to explain the reasoning behind all of the choices that were made in the implementation of the platform. The format may vary from team to team, but we want to capture the following points:

- **Background**: This is the history behind the decision to start the project. If the document will only be consumed internally, this can be pretty short. If it's going to be consumed externally, this is an opportunity to provide organizational context for your vendors and partners.
- **Executive summary**: This is really just a detailed summary of the entire document. Typically, this part of the deliverable will be used by managers, technology, and business leaders to understand the business impact of the overall recommendation. Requirements and the resulting architecture should be summarized.
- **Requirements**: This is the meat of the document. Requirements can be in whatever format is acceptable for your project management team. We prefer the "user story" format and will use that in the examples in this book.
- **Physical architecture**: This is an explanation of roles and physical machines which take those roles. This should include a network diagram.
- **Service architecture**: This is a summary of available services and their relationships. This section should include a service diagram.

- **Tenant architecture**: A section should be included which describes the expected landscape inside the cloud. This includes things such as available compute flavors, images, identity management architecture, and IPAM or DDI.
- **Roadmap**: This section is optional and often lives in another document. It's an opportunity to identify areas for improvement in future releases of the platform.

The design document often goes through a number of revisions as the project is developed. An important step at the end of each iteration of the platform is to reconcile any changes made to the platform with the design document.

 Beware of scope creep in the design document. This artifact has a tendency to turn into documentation on how OpenStack works. Remember to focus on explaining the decisions you made instead of what all the available options at the time were.

The deployment plan

Every implementation of OpenStack should start with a deployment plan. The design document describes what's being deployed and why, while the deployment plan describes how. Like the design document, the content of a deployment plan varies from organization to organization. It should at least include the following:

- **Hardware**: This is a list of the compute, storage, and network hardware available for the deployment.
- **Network addressing**: This is a table of IP and MAC addresses for the network assets in the deployment. For deployments of hundreds of compute nodes, this should probably be limited to a set of VLANs and subnets available for the deployment.
- **Deployment-specific configuration**: We'll assume that the configuration of the OpenStack deployment is automated. These are any settings that an engineer would need to adjust before launching the automated deployment of the environment.
- **Requirements**: These are things that need to be in place before the deployment can proceed. Normally, this is hardware configuration, switch configuration, LUN masking, and so on.

A good deployment plan will document everything that an engineering team needs to know to take the design document and instantiate it in the physical world. One thing that we like to leave out of the deployment plan is step-by-step instructions on how to deploy OpenStack. That information typically lives in an Installation Guide, which may be provided by a vendor or written by the operations team.

Your first OpenStack deployment

In our experience, almost all organizations approach OpenStack with the following three steps:

1. An individual, usually a Linux or Cloud Architect, installs OpenStack on a single machine to verify that the software can be deployed without too much effort.
2. The Architect enlists the help of other team members, typically Network and Storage Architects or Engineers to deploy a multiple-node installation. This will leverage some kind of shared ephemeral or block storage.
3. A team of Architects or Engineers craft the first deployment of OpenStack which is customized for the organization's use cases or environmental concerns. Professional services from a company such as Red Hat, Mirantis, HP, IBM, Canonical or Rackspace are often engaged at this point in the process.

From here on out, it's off to the races. We'll follow a similar pattern in this book. In this first chapter, we'll start with the first step-the "all-in-one" deployment.

Writing the initial deployment plan

Taking the time to document the very first deployment might seem a bit obsessive, but it provides us with the opportunity to begin iterating on the documentation that is the key to successful OpenStack deployments. We'll start with the following template.

Hardware

The initial deployment of OpenStack will leverage a single commodity server, a HP DL380.

Hostname	Model	CPU cores	Memory	Disk	Network
openstack	DL380	16	256 GB	500 GB	2 x 10 GB

This deployment provides compute capacity for 60 m1.medium instances or 30 m1.large instances.

Change the specifications in the table to meet your deployment. It's important to specify the expected capacity in the deployment document. For a basic rule of thumb, just divide the amount of available system memory by the instance memory. We'll talk more about accurately forecasting capacity in a later chapter.

Network addressing

There is one physical provider network in this deployment. SDN is provided in the tenant space by Neutron with the OVS ML2 plugin.

Hostname	MAC	IP
openstack	3C:97:0E:BF:6C:78	192.168.0.10

Change the network addresses in this section to meet your deployment. We'll only use a single network interface for the all-in-one installation.

Configuration notes

This deployment will use the RDO all-in-one reference architecture. This reference architecture uses a minimum amount of hardware as the basis for a monolithic installation of OpenStack, typically only used for testing or experimentation. For more information on the all-in-one deployment, refer to https://www.rdoproject.org/Quickstart.

For the first deployment, we'll just use the RDO distribution of the box. In later chapters, we'll begin to customize our deployment and we'll add notes to this section to describe where we've diverged from the reference architecture.

Requirements

The host system will need to meet the following requirements prior to deployment:

- Red Hat Enterprise Linux 7 (or CentOS 7)
- Network Manager must be disabled
- Network interfaces must be configured as per the **Network Addressing** section in /etc/sysconfig/network-scripts
- The RDO OpenStack repository must be enabled (from https://rdoproject.org /)

To enable the RDO repository, run the following command as the root user on your system:

```
yum install -y https://rdoproject.org/repos/rdo-release.rpm
```

Installing OpenStack

Assuming that we've correctly configured our host machine as per our deployment plan, the actual deployment of OpenStack is relatively straightforward. The installation instructions can either be captured in an additional section of the deployment plan or they can be captured in a separate document-the Installation Guide. Either way, the installation instructions should be immediately followed by a set of tests that can be run to verify that the deployment went correctly.

Installation instructions

To install OpenStack, execute the following command as the root user on the system designated in the deployment plan:

```
# yum install -y openstack-packstack
```

This command will install the packstack installation utility on the machine. If this command fails, ensure that the RDO repository is correctly enabled using the following command:

```
# rpm -q rdo-release
```

If the RDO repository has not been enabled, enable it using the following command:

```
# yum install -y https://rdoproject.org/repos/rdo-release.rpm
```

Next, run the `packstack` utility to install OpenStack:

```
# packstack --allinone
```

The `packstack` utility configures and applies a set of puppet manifests to your system to install and configure the OpenStack distribution. The `allinone` option instructs `packstack` to configure the set of services defined in the reference architecture for RDO.

Verifying the installation

Once the installation has completed successfully, use the following steps to verify the installation.

First, verify the Keystone identity service by attempting to get an authorization token. The OpenStack command-line client uses a set of environment variables to authenticate your session. Two configuration files which set those variables will be created by the `packstack` installation utility.

The `keystonerc_admin` file can be used to authenticate an administrative user and the `keystonerc_demo` file can be used to authenticate a nonprivileged user. An example `keystonerc` is shown as follows:

```
export OS_USERNAME=demo
export OS_TENANT_NAME=demo
export OS_PASSWORD=<random string>
export OS_AUTH_URL=http://192.168.0.10:5000/v2.0/
export PS1='[\u@\h \W(keystone_demo)]\$ '
```

This file will be used to populate your command-line session with the necessary environment variables and credentials that will allow you to communicate with the OpenStack APIs that use the Keystone service for authentication.

In order to use the `keystonerc` file to load your credentials, source the contents into your shell session from the directory you ran the `packstack` command. It will provide no output except for a shell prompt change:

```
# . ./keystonerc_demo
```

Your command prompt will change to remind you that you're using the sourced OpenStack credentials.

In order to load these credentials, the preceding source command must be run every time a user logs in. These credentials are not persistent. If you do not source your credentials before running OpenStack commands, you will most likely get the following error:

```
You must provide a username via either --os-username or
env[OS_USERNAME]
```

To verify the Keystone service, run the following command to get a Keystone token:

```
# openstack token issue
```

The output of this command should be a table similar to the following one:

```
+-----------+----------------------------------+
| Property  |               Value              |
+-----------+----------------------------------+
| expires   |        2015-07-14T05:01:41Z      |
| id        | a20264cd091847ac965cde8cbba7b0b9 |
| tenant_id | 202bd2fa2a3a40639bb0bccc9a57e37d |
| user_id   | 68d90544e0064c4c838d47d80811b895 |
+-----------+----------------------------------+
```

Next, verify the Glance image service:

```
# openstack image list
```

This should output a table listing a single image, the CirrOS image that is installed with the `packstack` command. We'll use the ID of that glance image to verify the Nova Compute service. Before we do that, we'll verify the Neutron Network service:

```
# openstack network list
```

This should output a table listing a network available to use for testing. We'll use the ID of that network to verify the Nova Compute service with the following commands:

First, add root's SSH key to OpenStack as `demo.key`:

```
# openstack keypair create --public-key ~/.ssh/id_rsa.pub demo
```

Now, create an instance called `instance01`:

```
# openstack server create --flavor m1.tiny \
--image <image_id> \
--key-name demo
--nic net-id=<networkid> \
instance01
```

This command will create the instance and output a table of information about the instance that you've just created. To check the status of the instance as it is provisioned, use the following command:

```
# openstack server show instance01
```

When the status becomes `ACTIVE`, the instance has successfully launched. The key created with the `nova keypair-add` command (`demo.key`) can be used to log into the instance once its running.

Next steps

At this point, you should have a working OpenStack installation on a single machine. To familiarize yourself with the OpenStack Horizon user interface, see the documentation on the RDO project website at `https://www.rdoproject.org/Running_an_instance`.

Summary

This chapter provided background information on OpenStack and the component services which make up an OpenStack deployment. We looked at some typical use cases for OpenStack and discussed the role of the Cloud Architect in an organization which is embarking on an OpenStack private cloud deployment.

We also began the documentation for our OpenStack deployments. The following documents were created:

- Deployment plan
- Installation guide

Finally, we completed an "all-in-one" OpenStack installation on a single server and verified the core set of services. This installation can be used to familiarize yourself with the OpenStack system. In the next chapter, we'll break down the different areas of design for OpenStack clouds and expand our documentation and deployment.

References

- https://www.openstack.org/summit/vancouver-2015/summit-videos/presentation/walmart-and-039s-cloud-journey
- https://www.openstack.org/summit/vancouver-2015/summit-videos/presentation/ceph-at-cern-a-year-in-the-life-of-a-petabyte-scale-block-storage-service
- https://www.openstack.org/user-stories/
- http://superuser.openstack.org/articles/openstack-user-survey-insights-november-2014
- http://blogs.gartner.com/thomas_bittman/2014/09/12/why-are-private-clouds-failing
- https://www.openstack.org/marketplace/public-clouds/rackspace/rackspace-public-cloud
- http://www.cybera.ca
- http://superuser.openstack.org/articles/openstack-users-share-how-their-deployments-stack-up

2
Architecting the Cloud

The array of possible hardware and software combinations that can be used to create an OpenStack cloud is pretty amazing at this point. A phrase we typically hear these days is that having an integration for OpenStack is "table stakes" for a hardware or software product coming in the market. As of the Liberty release of OpenStack (November 2015), there were over 50 Cinder storage drivers and 20 Neutron network drivers. These cover a wide range of products from traditional EMC storage arrays and Cisco switches to various software-defined storage and networking products. OpenStack supports a number of hypervisors and compute platforms ranging from commodity x86 hardware to IBM Z-series mainframes.

Few of the decisions we make as architects affect the bottom line as much as hardware and software selection. While we approach the deployment of our cloud or the development of our software in an iterative fashion to reduce the risk of mistakes, it is typically very difficult to iteratively purchase hardware.

Luckily, OpenStack ships with a set of **reference** plugins for each of the subsystems that we can use to mock out our cloud before purchasing actual hardware. For Cinder, the reference implementation involves using LVM and iSCSI on a Linux system. For Neutron, the reference implementation uses Open vSwitch and iptables on a Linux system. Even Compute can be mocked out using nested virtualization with KVM. The approach that we recommend is to begin an OpenStack project with the reference plugins until you get a feel of how the software and hardware will work together before making any large hardware or software purchases.

Picking an OpenStack distribution

OpenStack is developed like most open source software projects. The code is available at `ht tp://openstack.org` and can be downloaded in the package format from `http://tarball s .openstack.org`. As of the Liberty release of OpenStack, there were over 350 individual projects available for download. That's a huge number of source repositories for an engineering team to sort through and manage. Hence the development of the OpenStack distributions. Most of the OpenStack distributions are put together by the same groups that put together Linux distributions. For example, the three major distributions available are part of the Ubuntu, openSUSE, and CentOS Linux distributions. Each of these distributions maintain installation guides, available at `http://docs.openstack.org`. There are also distributions available from companies such as HP, Mirantis, and Red Hat which are part of commercial support agreements. In addition to these options, there are also companies such as Platform9, which provide managed OpenStack deployments.

Running from the trunk

As we mentioned before, stable releases of OpenStack happen on a six-month cadence. Active development happens in the trunk of each of the software projects (the "master" branch on the web-based repository service for OpenStack at `http://git.openstack.org`). This master repository controls the distributed version control for the OpenStack project and aids in source code management. This is very similar to the well-known GitHub service used by many other open source projects. In addition to the Git repository, there are some number of **stable** branches corresponding to the six-month releases. Features are implemented in the master branch and bug fixes are backported from the trunk to the branches on an irregular basis.

For most organizations, taking a packaged version of one of the stable branches and deploying it will suffice. There are a couple of reasons why this might not be appealing, though. For one, some organizations might find that too much change accumulates between the six-month releases and that there's less risk in releasing more frequent and smaller changes from the trunk. While this makes sense with a lot of software projects, OpenStack is developed by a number of loosely coordinated teams and managing the dependencies between the development streams of each project is a complicated task. Automated testing on the trunk attempts to ensure that a change in Nova doesn't break a feature in Neutron, but the bulk of manual integration testing happens for the coordinated stable releases.

While it's possible that an organization may want to take all the changes from trunk before they make it down to the stable branches, it's more likely that they'll be interested in only one or two important features that haven't made it to the branches. For example, many of the teams that we have worked with were interested in leveraging external IPAM systems similar to the one provided by Infoblox long before the feature was implemented in Neutron (in the Liberty release). We've seen other situations in which an organization wanted to pull in a Cinder driver for a new SAN device before it was accepted upstream. For these use cases, it makes more sense to start off with a packaged distribution of one of the stable branches and then create a custom package only for the component which has the desired feature backported to it from the trunk.

Community distributions

After each stable release of OpenStack, the software from the resulting stable branches is packaged up by maintainers from three of the major community Linux distributions into the native format for their distribution. These distributions of OpenStack allow users of those distributions to install the software (and its dependencies) using the usual mechanism for that distribution. These distributors also provide documentation at `http://openstack.org` on how to install and configure the software on their particular distribution.

Most organizations will choose a community distribution based on the Linux distribution that they're the most comfortable with. For example, organizations which typically use the Ubuntu Linux distribution will use the Ubuntu OpenStack distribution as well. It's worth noting that the community distributions of OpenStack will work with the commercially supported variants of both openSUSE and CentOS; it's not uncommon for an organization to pay for support for Red Hat Enterprise Linux but to use the community-supported CentOS distribution of OpenStack (RDO).

The choice of community distribution may also have an effect on the availability of installation mechanisms. For example, the Packstack installation tool that we used in `Chapter 1`, *Introducing OpenStack*, is specific to the CentOS distribution of OpenStack (RDO). The Ubuntu and openSUSE distributions have other tools for installing the OpenStack software. However, the Puppet, Chef, and Ansible mechanisms for deploying OpenStack are distribution (and operating system) agnostic. For example, it is possible to deploy OpenStack on the Ubuntu and CentOS distributions using the same Puppet modules.

Commercially supported distributions

While there are only three major community-supported distributions of OpenStack available, there are a myriad of commercially-supported distributions available. A list of these distributions and their certification status is available at `http://openstack.org`. Distributions which have passed specific load and performance-based **Tempest** tests are certified in the same way as managed service providers. Commercially-supported distributions are frequently based on the community-supported distributions. However, there are a few reasons that organizations prefer them to the community distributions.

The first major driver is support. Most companies which provide support for OpenStack require the customer to use their commercially supported distribution so that they can ensure that the customer is using software which has passed through a certification and testing process. For example, Red Hat takes the packages from each RDO release and runs them through a detailed test plan before releasing them as Red Hat Enterprise Linux OpenStack platform. When a customer identifies an issue with a particular OpenStack component, Red Hat can add that issue to the test plan to prevent regressions in future releases. Additionally customers may choose different commercial distributions for ease of use, quality of support, or any additional software that may be included with the distribution; for example, Hewlett Packard Enterprise's Helion OpenStack is bundled with a number of operational tools that may appeal to some customers. Mirantis OpenStack, while only an **Information as a Service (IaaS)** platform, has an installer that some customers may prefer over other distribution's installers.

Organizations may also choose a commercially-supported distribution over a community-supported distribution because the distribution has added functionality that hasn't been released by the distributor as open source. For example, IBM has an OpenStack distribution within their IBM Cloud Manager offering. These enhancements tend to be aimed toward speeding the deployment of OpenStack clouds or improving the manageability of deployments with additional reporting and dashboards.

Compute hardware considerations

It's certainly possible to deploy OpenStack on Power or Z series systems from IBM or Solaris systems from Oracle, but the vast majority of OpenStack deployments use Linux on 64-bit Intel systems. Selecting a hardware platform for compute infrastructure in OpenStack is similar to selecting a hardware platform for any other workload in the data center. Some organizations have a brand loyalty to a particular vendor based on reputation, past performance, or business arrangements and some organizations ask hardware vendors to bid on projects as they come up. A small number of organizations choose to assemble their own systems from components, but most OpenStack deployments use the same commodity systems that would be deployed to run any other Linux workload.

With that said, we've definitely seen hardware configurations that work well with OpenStack and ones which had to be reconfigured after the fact. We'll try to help you avoid that second purchase order in this section.

Hypervisor selection

The majority of installations use either the Xen or KVM hypervisors, but there are a number of other hypervisors available for use with Nova. Both the Hyper-V and VMware hypervisors are supported as compute platforms. Bare-metal systems can be provisioned via Nova (Ironic project) and various drivers for containers have come and gone over the life of OpenStack. Running containers in OpenStack is a topic of great interest lately and the OpenStack Magnum project has emerged as the current favorite model for their deployment within OpenStack.

Whether to pick the Xen or KVM hypervisor is almost a religious matter for some people. The KVM hypervisor is the most broadly used hypervisor on Linux and it has support for a wide range of advanced features such as PCI-passthrough, NUMA zone pinning, and live migration. Proponents of Xen will point out that performance on older hardware has traditionally been better with Xen. They will also point out that large cloud providers such as Amazon and Rackspace have picked the Xen hypervisor over the KVM hypervisor for their deployments. However, adoption continues to wane for the Xen hypervisor. Based on the 2016 OpenStack User Survey report, 95% of OpenStack clouds are using KVM and only 4% are using Xen. KVM is the default and most widely used hypervisor, and unless your organization has a strong motivation to pick the Xen hypervisor, we strongly recommend that you use it over any other hypervisor.

A number of good arguments can be made for using VMware ESX as the hypervisor in OpenStack instead of KVM. Almost every large IT shop has a great deal of experience with ESX and vSphere and using ESX as the hypervisor for an OpenStack deployment can ease the barrier for entry to OpenStack for teams which don't want to certify or train up on a new virtualization technology. ESX-based deployments are prescriptive-there is only one Cinder driver and one Neutron driver supported with ESX. From this perspective, choosing ESX allows an organization to focus on the integration and operational aspects of OpenStack without worrying too much about the architecture.

The same reasons that make ESX a good choice for some organizations make it a poor choice for most organizations, though. The prescriptive approach limits available options in the storage and network space. One of the strongest aspects of OpenStack is the heterogeneity of the ecosystem and the ability to dynamically add new types of infrastructure under a common API. For this reason, we'll be focusing our work in this book on the use of the KVM hypervisor. Most of the considerations we address in this section will also apply to the Xen hypervisor.

Sizing the hardware to match the workload

As we mentioned at the start of this chapter, while an iterative approach for developing and deploying software is a best practice, an iterative approach for purchasing hardware has the potential to kill your private cloud initiative. It's crucial to get the hardware right the first time so that you can line up the appropriate discounts from your hardware vendor and set the appropriate budget at the start of the project. Sizing is often difficult for these projects though, as it can be difficult to anticipate the requirements of the workload ahead of time. This is one of the reasons that it's so important to get the application owners involved early in the project-they'll be able to anticipate what their application requirements will be and that will inform the sizing process.

The first step in the sizing process is to define standard instance sizes. These are referred to as **flavors** in the Nova parlance. Out of the box, Nova ships with a set of **m1** flavors, which correspond roughly to Amazon EC2 instance types. A flavor has three prominent parameters, the number of virtual CPUs, the amount of memory, and the amount of ephemeral disk storage. Organizations typically define two or three flavors, based on anticipated workload. Three common flavors are the 1×2, 2×4, and 4×8 sizes, which refer to the number of vCPUs and gigabytes of memory. The ephemeral disk size is typically the same, regardless of CPU and memory configuration-it should equate to the expected size of a **root** disk of the organization's standard Glance images. For example, a 2×4 with the Red Hat Enterprise Linux 7 qcow2 image would have two virtual CPUs, four gigabytes of memory, and a 20 gigabyte ephemeral disk.

Once the flavors have been defined, the next step is to determine the acceptable over-commit ratio for a given environment. Each of the major hardware vendors publishes virtual performance benchmark results that can be used as a starting point for this ratio. These benchmarks are available at `http://spec.org/` in the **Virtualization** category. Working through these benchmarks, two simple rules emerge: never over-commit memory and always over-commit CPU up to 10 times. Following these rules allows you to determine the optimal amount of memory in a given piece of compute hardware. For example, a compute node with 36 physical cores can support up to 360 virtual cores of compute. If we use the preceding flavors, we'll see a ratio of two gigabytes of RAM to each virtual core. The optimum amount of memory in this compute node would top out somewhere around 720 GB (2 GB x 10 x 36 cores).

There's typically a dramatic price difference in tiers of memory and it often makes sense to configure the system with less than the optimum amount of memory. Let's assume that it is only economical to configure our 36 core compute node with 512 GB of memory. The next two items to consider are network bandwidth and available ephemeral storage. This is where it helps to understand the target workload. 512 GB of memory would support 256 1×2 instances, 128 2×4 instances, or 64 4×8 instances. That gives us a maximum ephemeral disk requirement between 1.2 and 5 TB, assuming a 20 GB Glance image. That's a pretty large discrepancy. If we feel confident that the bulk of our instances will be 2x4s, we can size for around 128 instances, which gives us a requirement of 2.5 TB of disk for ephemeral storage. There's some leeway in there as well-ephemeral storage is thin-provisioned with the KVM hypervisor and it's unlikely that we'll consume the full capacity. However, if we use persistent storage options such as Ceph, SAN, iSCSI, or NFS for image, instance or object storage, planning for capacity becomes more complicated. While determining your flavor CPU, memory, and ephemeral disk sizing, you will need to include persistent disk space for root volumes. If these volumes are stored on the same appliances/clusters as your glance and object storage, great care must be taken to ensure consistent elasticity.

The last major item to consider when selecting compute hardware is the available bandwidth on the compute node. Most of the systems we work with today have two 10 gigabit bonded interfaces dedicated to instance traffic. Dividing the available bandwidth by the number of anticipated instances allows us to determine whether an additional set of interfaces is required. Dividing 10 gigabits by 128 instances gives us roughly 75 megabits of available average bandwidth for each instance. This is more than sufficient for most web and database workloads.

Considerations for performance-intensive workloads

The guidelines given earlier work well for development, web, or database workloads. Some workloads, particularly **Network Function Virtualization** (**NFV**) workloads, have very specific performance requirements that need to be addressed in the hardware selection process. A few improvements to the scheduling of instances have recently been added to the Nova compute service in order to enable these workloads.

 NFV is a new developing use case for OpenStack to be used to be the infrastructure for workloads that would replace dedicated network appliances. Routers, firewalls, proxy servers, and packet core devices are some of the common virtual network functions that are being replaced today. Not only does NFV reduce the physical hardware needed to operate telecommunication businesses but it also brings all of the benefits of cloud native application orchestration to a business case that has an increasing need for agility to supply consumers with services faster than ever.

The first improvement allows for passing through a PCI device directly from the hardware into the instance. In standard OpenStack Neutron networking, packets traverse a set of bridges between the instance's virtual interface and the actual network interface. The amount of overhead in this virtual networking is significant, as each packet consumes CPU resources each time it traverses an interface or switch. This performance overhead can be eliminated by allowing the virtual machine to have direct access to the network device via a technology called SR-IOV. SR-IOV allows a single network adapter to appear as multiple network adapters to the operating system. Each of these virtual network adapters (referred to as virtual functions, or VFs) can be directly associated with a virtual instance.

The second improvement allows the Nova scheduler to specify the CPU and memory zone for an instance on a compute node which has **Non-Uniform Memory Access** (**NUMA**). In these NUMA systems, a certain amount of memory is located closer to a certain set of processor cores. A performance penalty occurs when processes access memory pages in a region which is nonadjacent. Another significant performance penalty occurs when processes move from one memory zone to another. To get around these performance penalties, the Nova scheduler has the ability to **pin** the virtual CPUs of an instance to physical cores in the underlying compute node. It also has the ability to restrict a virtual instance to a given memory region associated with those virtual CPUs, effectively constraining the instance to a specified NUMA zone.

The last major performance improvement in the Nova Compute service is around memory page allocation. By default, the Linux operating system allocates memory in 4 kilobyte pages on 64-bit Intel systems. While this makes a lot of sense for traditional workloads (it maps to the size of a typical filesystem block), it can have an adverse effect on memory allocation performance in virtual machines. The Linux operating system also allows for 2 megabyte and 1 gigabyte sized memory pages, commonly referred to as **huge pages**. The Kilo release of OpenStack included support for using huge pages to back virtual instances.

The combination of PCI-passthrough, CPU and memory pinning, and huge page support allow dramatic performance improvements for virtual instances in OpenStack and are required for workloads such as NFV. They have some implications for hardware selection that are worth noting, though. Typical NFV instances will expect to have an entire NUMA zone dedicated to them. As such, these are typically very large flavors and the flavors tend to be application-specific. They're also hardware-specific-if your flavor specifies that the instance needs 16 virtual CPUs and 32 gigabytes of memory, then the hardware needs to have a NUMA zone with 16 physical cores and 32 gigabytes of memory available. Also, if that NUMA zone has an addition 32 gigabytes of memory configured, it will be unavailable to the rest of the system as the instance has exclusive access to that zone.

Network design

The network requirements for a particular OpenStack deployment also vary widely depending on the workload. OpenStack also typically provides an organization's first experience with **Software-Defined Networking** (**SDN**), which complicates the design process for the physical and virtual networks. Cloud Architects should lean heavily on their peers in the Network Architecture team in the planning of the network.

Providing network segmentation

OpenStack's roots in the public cloud provider space have left a significant impact on the network design at both the physical and virtual layer. In a public cloud deployment, the relationship between the tenant workload and the provider workload is based on a total absence of trust. In these deployments, the users and applications in the tenant space have no network access to any of the systems which are providing the underlying compute, network, and storage. Some access has to be provided for the end users to reach the API endpoints of the OpenStack cloud though, and so the control plane is typically multihomed on a set of physically segmented networks. This adds a layer of complexity to the deployment, but it has proven to be a best practice from a security standpoint in private cloud deployments as well.

There are typically four types of networks in an OpenStack deployment. The first is a network which is used to access the OpenStack APIs from the Internet in the case of a public cloud, or the intranet in the case of a private cloud. In most deployments, only the load balancers have an address on this network. This allows for tight control and auditing of traffic coming in from the Internet. This network is often referred to as the **External** network. The second type of network is a private network which is used for communication between the OpenStack control plane and the compute infrastructure. The message bus and database are exposed on this network and traffic is typically not routed in or out of this network. This network is referred to as the **Management** network.

Two more additional private networks are typically created to carry network and storage traffic between the compute, network, and storage nodes. These networks are broken out for quality of service as much as security and are optional, depending on whether or not the deployment is using SDN or network-attached storage. The segment dedicated to tenant networking is frequently referred to as the **Tenant** network or the **Underlay** network. Depending on the size of the deployment, there may be one or more of these underlay networks. The storage network is, not surprisingly, referred to as the **Storage** network.

One last class of network is required for tenant workloads to access the Internet or intranet in most deployments. Commonly referred to as the **Provider** network, this is a physical network which is modeled in Neutron to provide network ports on a physical network. Floating IPs which can be dynamically assigned to instances are drawn from the Provider networks. In some deployments, instances will be allowed to use ports from Provider networks directly, without passing through the Tenant network and router. Organizations which would like to have the Neutron API available, but don't want to implement SDN frequently use this pattern of modeling the physical infrastructure in Neutron with provider networks.

This allows them to use traditional physical switches and routers but still provide dynamic virtual interfaces.

Reference Architectures, Fuel 7.0 Reference, Mirantis `https://docs.mirantis.com/fuel/fuel-7.0/reference-architecture.html`

SDN

SDN is one of the key capabilities that differentiates OpenStack from traditional virtualization deployments. SDN uses tunneling technology to create a virtual network topology on top of a physical network topology. The virtual (overlay) networks can be shared or tenant-specific. Tenants can define their own layer 2 segments and routers, they can specify network-specific DNS and DHCP services, and some deployments allow for layer 4 services such as load balancing and firewalling to be defined as well. Neutron was created with a plugin-based architecture and plugins exist for software and hardware-based SDN products. A reference implementation built around Open vSwitch is also provided for testing and lab work.

Selecting an SDN provider is a difficult task. In our experience, SDN vendors tend to obfuscate their technology with marketing terms and it takes a while to figure out exactly how each vendor is actually routing packets through the hypervisor out to the physical networks. Many of the early Neutron SDN plugins like Nicira's were based on the Open vSwitch software which Nicira authored. The performance of these solutions was poor and a number of different approaches have since moved the processing of packets from the "user space" in the Linux operating system down into the "kernel space". Work has also been done towards improving the performance of the reference Open vSwitch implementation by simplifying the path that packets take from the instance down through the switches. This project is called Open Virtual Network, or OVN.

SDN vendors tend to differentiate themselves in three areas. The first is around the resiliency of their solution. Organizations evaluating SDN technologies should pay attention to how the layer 3 routers are made highly available in a given topology and how packet flows are impacted by component failure. The second is around the management interface of a given solution. Most of the SDN vendors will have an eye-catching and useful user interface to use to debug packet flows within the tenant networks. The third factor to consider is performance. In our experience, this is the deciding factor for most organizations. There are typically large differences in the performance of these solutions and attention should be focused on this during **Proof of Concepts (POCs)**.

Physical network design

No discussion of OpenStack networking would be complete without the mention of the **spine-leaf** physical network architecture. Spine-leaf is an alternative to the traditional **multi-tier** network architecture which is made up of a set of core, aggregation, and access layers. Spine-leaf introduces a modification to the design of the aggregation layer in order to reduce the number of hops between servers which are attached to different access switches. The aggregation layer becomes a **spine,** in which every access switch (the **leaf)** can reach every other access switch through a single spine switch. This architecture is considered a prerequisite for horizontally scalable cloud workloads, which are focused more on traffic between instances (east-west traffic) than traffic between instances and the Internet (north-south traffic).

The primary impact that spine-leaf network design has on OpenStack deployments is that layer 2 networks are typically terminated at the spine – meaning that subnets cannot stretch from leaf to leaf. This has a couple of implications. First, virtual IPs cannot migrate from leaf to leaf and thus the External network is constrained to a single leaf. If the leaf boundary is the top-of-rack switch, this places all of the load balancers for a given control plane within a single failure zone (the rack). Second, Provider networks need to be physically attached to each compute node within an OpenStack region *if instances are going to be directly attached to them.* This limitation can constrain an OpenStack region to the size of a leaf. Once again, if the leaf boundary is the top-of-rack switch, this makes for very small regions, which lead to an unusually high ratio of control to compute nodes.

We've seen a couple of different approaches on how to implement spine-leaf within OpenStack installations given these limitations. The first is to simply stretch L2 networks across the leaves in a given deployment. The only networks which require stretching are the External API network and the Provider networks. If instances are not going to be directly attached to the Provider networks (that is, if floating IPs are used for external connectivity), then these networks only need to be stretched across a failure zone to ensure that the loss of a single rack doesn't bring down the control plane. Deployments which chose to stretch L2 across racks typically group racks into **pods** of three or more racks which then become the leaf boundary. The second approach that we've seen used is to create tunnels within the spine which simulate stretched L2 subnets across the top of rack switches. Either way, collaboration between the network architecture team and the cloud architecture team should lead to a solution which is supportable by the organization.

Floating IPs are pools of IP addresses that are typically external facing and can be attached and detached to running instances at will to provide external access to the instance. These floating IP addresses are associated with a tenant router and are dynamically assigned.

Storage design

As compute hardware has become less expensive over the last few years, fewer and fewer workloads are constrained by a lack of processor or memory performance. Instead, most workloads are tuned so that they are constrained on I/O-particularly storage I/O. OpenStack workloads typically separate the operating system storage from the application storage and Cinder and the different object storage projects provide mechanisms for presenting many different kinds of storage with a single interface. This capability allows tenants to choose the storage which matches their application's requirements. In addition to Cinder providing persistence for applications, block storage and object storage also provide storage persistence for instances and allow for instance live migration, backup, and recovery.

Ephemeral storage

Ephemeral storage is the storage that is consumed when a Glance image is copied locally to a compute node to instantiate a virtual instance. Glance images are typically sparse and tend to be less than one gigabyte in size. When instantiated, images provide the **root** disk for an instance's operating system. These are also sparsely provisioned, but typically grow up to 10, 20, or 40 gigabytes in size. In traditional OpenStack deployments, ephemeral storage is provided by the compute node's internal disks, and when a compute node fails or an instance is terminated, the storage is lost or reclaimed. These days, many organizations will chose to place ephemeral storage on shared storage though.

There are two main reasons to use shared storage for ephemeral instance storage. The first reason is to make those ephemeral instances a little less ephemeral by providing for a live-migration capability for instances. With local-only ephemeral storage, any reboot of a compute node will terminate the instances it is currently hosting. If the instance is backed by shared storage (typically NFS or software-based storage such as Ceph), it can be migrated to another compute node which has access to the same storage without downtime. This allows for cloud operators to put compute nodes in a "maintenance mode" so that they can be patched. When the compute nodes are ready to host workloads again, the instances can be rebalanced across the nodes. Having a live copy of the instance is also useful in the case of a compute node failure. Instances backed by shared storage can be evacuated to healthy compute nodes without losing state.

The second reason that shared storage is attractive for ephemeral storage is that some storage backends allow for deduplication between Glance images and running instances. In a traditional instance life cycle, there isn't a huge need for deduplication between the images and the instances. However, if there is a deduplication capability, it allows for operators to use instance snapshots as backups. Instances can be backed up on a regular basis without consuming an inordinate amount of shared storage. New features in the Kilo and Liberty releases of OpenStack allow for quiescing guest operating systems during snapshot operations to enable this kind of "live backup" capability.

Block storage

Using shared storage for ephemeral storage is one way to achieve a persistence capability for virtual instances, but the more traditional way is to instantiate a Glance image on a Cinder volume. Instances which are backed by Cinder volumes can be live-migrated, live-snapshotted, and evacuated with their state intact. There are Cinder drivers for almost every major storage product on the market these days and it is common to configure multiple backends within a single OpenStack deployment. This allows the OpenStack tenant to chose an appropriate backend for their workload. For example, a database instance might have its operating system reside on relatively inexpensive ephemeral disk, but locate the data on highly performant SAN storage attached by fiber channel. If the instance fails, the root disk is discarded and a new instance attaches itself to the persistent Cinder volume. Cinder volumes are also attractive as root disks for instances which are being migrated from traditional virtualization platforms. The user experience for Cinder-backed instances is very similar to these platforms.

Selection of storage backends for Cinder implementations is a relatively straightforward process. Cloud Architects will want to leverage the relationships and knowledge that an organization's Storage Architects already have. Storage devices are relatively expensive and POCs should be run on existing hardware devices where possible. Cinder drivers for commonplace devices such as NetApp filers and EMC SANs have some interesting features which can be proven out in a lab. Vendors of more exotic hardware devices are typically willing to lend hardware for POCs as well.

Most of the organizations that we've worked with have tested software-based storage as a part of their OpenStack implementations and many have gone on to adopt software-based storage for at least one of their storage tiers. Ceph, in particular, has a tight integration with OpenStack for image, ephemeral, and block storage. Ceph has the advantage of providing deduplication when used in this configuration. This, combined with its usage of commodity hardware, makes it an extremely attractive option from a cost perspective.

Object storage

Swift was one of the first two services in OpenStack and object storage was the original mechanism for persistence within OpenStack (and Amazon) clouds. As OpenStack has been adopted for more and more traditional workloads, object storage has lost a lot of its relevance. In fact, many of the OpenStack deployments that we work on in the Enterprise space don't include object storage in the initial release.

An easy way to take an "if you build it they will come" approach to object storage is to leverage it for storing Glance images. While few of your tenants may come to your OpenStack deployment with applications that can persist their data over an S3-compatible interface, almost all of them can use the snapshot capability in Nova to improve their experience on the platform. Storing Glance images in Swift makes them highly available and provides an opportunity to co-locate them with the compute infrastructure, dramatically improving network performance.

Object storage backend selection is highly dependent on block and ephemeral storage selection. If you are using Ceph for block storage, using Ceph for object storage greatly simplifies administration of the platform. NetApp provides an integration with Swift, and it may be advantageous to choose it instead if using NetApp for block storage. Swift is also the default object storage provider in OpenStack and it makes sense to use it in heterogeneous environments from that perspective. In our experience, object storage backends are not subjected to the same kind of scrutiny as block storage backends in the storage selection process. This may be because many object storage systems are less about performance and more about low-cost options to store frequently read data versus a lot of heavy I/O.

Expanding the initial deployment

To properly evaluate the different compute, network, and storage options we've discussed in this chapter, an expanded OpenStack deployment with dedicated roles for different physical systems is required. Separating the compute functions from the control functions allows us to properly test different types of compute hardware. Separating storage functions from compute and control functions allows us to properly test different disk, NAS, or SAN configurations. In this section, we'll split out the roles we deployed in Chapter 1, *Introducing OpenStack*, to three physical systems. Each of these systems will be assigned a role, called a host group.

Updating the design document

Our first task is to update the design document from Chapter 1, *Introducing OpenStack*, with a set of definitions of our host groups. These definitions should be included at the start of the *Physical architecture* section of the document. We'll use the following host groups in this expanded **proof of concept** (**POC**).

Cloud controller

The cloud controller system provides the API services, scheduling services, and Horizon dashboard services for the OpenStack deployment.

Compute node

The compute node systems act as KVM hypervisors and run the nova-compute and openvswitch-agent services.

The *Physical architecture* section of the design document should also contain a section on the physical network architecture of the deployment. In this section, each of the segmented networks should be defined. Connectivity for each physical host to each network should also be defined.

The Packstack installation tool doesn't allow for the specification of an external network for API traffic. As such, we'll use three physical networks in this deployment, a management network which is routable to the intranet, a provider network which provides floating IPs for the instances, and a tenant network for instance traffic. The following network definitions should be added to the *Physical architecture* section.

Management network

The management network is used for the private communication between all nodes in the OpenStack deployment. This network is also used to carry tenant and storage traffic in this deployment.

Provider network

The provider network is used to provide public ports for tenant instances in this deployment. The cloud controller node has a port on this network segment.

Tenant network

The tenant network carries the tenant network traffic in the deployment. It acts as an underlay network for the SDN tunnels. Compute nodes and controller nodes have ports on this network segment.

A network diagram should also be added to the *Physical architecture* section. The following diagram describes the deployment in this chapter:

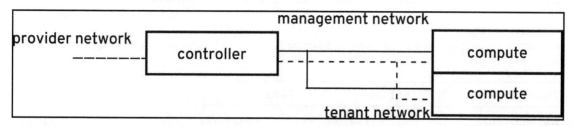

Updating the deployment plan

The deployment plan for our lab environment needs to be updated to reflect the additional hardware and network configuration. The hardware table should be updated first to include the assignment of role to each piece of hardware. For example, consider the following table:

Hostname	Model	CPU cores	Memory	Disk	Network	Host group
controller1	DL380	16	256 GB	500 GB	2×10 GB	Cloud controller
compute1	DL380	32	512 GB	2 TB	2×10 GB	Compute node
compute2	DL380	32	512 GB	2 TB	2×10 GB	Compute node

Next, update the network table to reflect the new nodes and networks:

Hostname	Interface	MAC	IP	Network
controller1	eth0	3C:97:0E:BF:6C:78	192.168.0.10	Management
	eth0.100	3C:97:0E:BF:6C:78	10.0.0.10	Provider
	eth0.200	3C:97:0E:BF:6C:78	172.16.0.10	Tenant
compute1	eth0	3C:97:0E:BF:6C:80	192.168.0.100	Management
	eth0.200	3C:97:0E:BF:6C:80	172.16.0.100	Tenant
compute2	eth0	3C:97:0E:BF:6C:81	192.168.0.101	Management
	eth0.200	3C:97:0E:BF:6C:81	172.16.0.101	Tenant

It can also be helpful to include a table like the following, which describes each network for the deployment:

Network	VLAN ID	Subnet	Gateway
Management		192.168.0.0/24	192.168.0.1
Provider	100	10.0.0.0/24	10.0.0.1
Tenant	200	172.16.0.0/24	172.16.0.1

Installing OpenStack with the new configuration

In Chapter 1, *Introducing OpenStack*, we ran packstack with the allinone option, taking the defaults for a test installation. Packstack has the ability to save the default options into a configuration file which can then be edited with a text editor. We'll use this ability in this chapter to create a reusable configuration. Also, packstack has the ability to apply the generated puppet manifests to remote machines over SSH. For this to work, you will need to be able to access SSH from the controller machine (where we'll be running packstack) to the other machines in the deployment. It's a good idea to test this out prior to running packstack.

To begin, start by installing a fresh copy of the operating system on the four servers that we outlined in the hardware table in the deployment plan. Each system needs to have the network interfaces specified in the network table configured before deployment and all of the requirements specified in the deployment plan will also need to be met(that is, Network Manager needs to be disabled and the RDO repository needs to be enabled).

Execute the following command on the cloud controller (`controller1`) to generate an answer file. We'll use this as a template for our deployment configuration:

```
# packstack --gen-answer-file=packstack-answers.txt
```

Next, edit the `packstack-answers.txt` file, updating the following parameters:

Parameter	Example	Description
CONFIG_CONTROLLER_HOST	192.168.0.10	IP address of the cloud controller on the management network
CONFIG_COMPUTE_HOSTS	192.168.0.100, 192.168.0.101	IP addresses of the compute nodes on the management network
CONFIG_NETWORK_HOSTS	192.168.0.10	IP address of the cloud controller on the management network
CONFIG_AMQP_HOST	192.168.0.10	IP address of the cloud controller on the management network
CONFIG_MARIADB_HOST	192.168.0.10	IP address of the cloud controller on the management network

CONFIG_NEUTRON_OVS_BRIDGE_MAPPINGS	vlan100:br-vlan100	A mapping of neutron networks to OVS bridges for the provider network
CONFIG_NEUTRON_OVS_BRIDGE_IFACES	br-vlan100:eth0.100	A mapping of OVS bridges to physical interfaces for the provider network
CONFIG_NEUTRON_OVS_TUNNEL_IF	eth0.200	An interface to use for the tenant network
CONFIG_PROVISION_DEMO_FLOATRANGE	10.0.0.128/25	A floating IP range to use on the provider network

A quick note on the Neutron settings, as they've always seemed confusing to us. The tunnel interface setting is used by the puppet module to determine the local_ip setting in the Open vSwitch plugin configuration file. The bridge mappings setting is the same as bridge_mappings in the Open vSwitch plugin configuration file. The bridge interfaces setting, however, doesn't effect the plugin configuration. Instead, it's used by the puppet module to determine how to construct the Open vSwitch bridge which is referred to by the bridge_mappings setting. If you intend to construct the bridge manually, it's safe to leave out that setting.

Now, run packstack with the new configuration:

```
# packstack --answer-file=packstack-answers.txt
```

When the installation completes, the OpenStack deployment should be verified using the same steps as in the previous chapter. Service distribution can be verified by querying the Nova and Neutron schedulers:

```
# nova service-list
```

This command will output a table of all running compute services, the host they're running on, and their status. The output should show the `nova-cert`, `nova-consoleauth`, `nova-scheduler`, and `nova-conductor` services as running on `compute1` and the `nova-compute` service as running on `compute1` and `compute2`.

```
# neutron agent-list
```

This command will output a similar table of all running network services. The output should show the Metadata, L3, and DHCP agents running on `controller1` and the Open vSwitch agent running on `controller1`, `compute1`, and `compute2`.

Summary

OpenStack deployments are often compared to snowflakes. There are so many different ways to combine the various supported compute, storage, and network configurations that no deployment resembles any other deployment. The analogy is frequently used in frustration at companies which offer commercial support for OpenStack – the diversity of deployments makes supporting customers extremely difficult. Many of the clients we work with have also expressed frustration at the myriad of options. On the other hand, most of the people who have been running OpenStack for a while realize the value in having so many options. It allows them to continually provide new services and capabilities to their customers under a common interface.

In this chapter, we walked through each of the three major areas of technology in OpenStack-compute, network, and storage. In each area, we've broadly described the choices available and provided some guidance on how to approach the decision process. We've also expanded our deployment documentation and the deployment itself to incorporate some of the information covered in this chapter. This basic deployment can be expanded and should provide enough diversity to be used to test out different compute, network, and storage technologies in the lab before making a purchasing decision.

In the next chapter, you'll look at how to take this simple deployment and make it more robust with the addition of high availability software.

References

- List of Neutron Plugins: `https://wiki.openstack.org/wiki/Neutron#Plugins`
- List of Cinder Drivers: `https://wiki.openstack.org/wiki/CinderSupportMatrix`
- List of OpenStack Distributions: `https://www.openstack.org/marketplace/distros/`
- Standard Performance Evaluation Comparison for Virtualization: `http://spec.org/virt_sc2013/`

3

Planning for Failure (and Success)

In this chapter, we'll be walking through how to architect your cloud to avoid hardware and software failures. The OpenStack control plane is comprised of web services, application services, database services, and a message bus. All of these tiers require different approaches to make them highly available and some organizations will already have defined architectures for each of the services. We've seen that customers either reuse those existing patterns or adopt new ones which are specific to the OpenStack platform. Both of these approaches make sense, depending on the scale of the deployment. Many successful deployments actually implement a blend of these.

For example, if your organization already has a supported pattern for highly available MySQL databases, you might chose that pattern instead of the one outlined in this chapter. If your organization doesn't have a pattern for highly available MongoDB, you might have to architect a new one.

This chapter is divided into the following topics:

- Highly available control plane strategies and patterns
- OpenStack regions, cells, and availability zones
- Updating the design document and implementing the design

Building a highly available control plane

Back in the Folsom and Grizzly days, coming up with an **High Availability (H/A)** design for the OpenStack control plane was something of a black art. Many of the technologies recommended in the first iterations of the OpenStack High Availability Guide were specific to the Ubuntu distribution of Linux and were unavailable on the Red Hat Enterprise Linux-derived distributions.

The now-standard cluster resource manager (Pacemaker) was unsupported by Red Hat at that time. As such, architects using Ubuntu might use one set of software, those using CentOS or RHEL might use another set of software, and those using a Rackspace or Mirantis distribution might use yet another set of software. However, these days, the technology stack has converged and the H/A pattern is largely consistent regardless of the distribution used.

About failure and success

When we design a highly available OpenStack control plane, we're looking to mitigate two different scenarios:

- The first is failure. When a physical piece of hardware dies, we want to make sure that we recover without human interaction and continue to provide service to our users.
- The second and perhaps more important scenario is success.

Software systems always work as designed and tested until humans start using them. While our automated test suites will try to launch a reasonable number of virtual objects, humans are guaranteed to attempt to launch an unreasonable number. Also, many of the OpenStack projects we've worked on have grown far past their expected size and need to be expanded on-the-fly.

One of the early Havana-based clouds we worked on used a memory-based fiber channel storage array as a Cinder backend. All of our automated testing for the platform succeeded, but within a week of handing it over, we were told that the operators couldn't launch virtual instances. Our automated unit tests continued to succeed, but the manual testing the operators were doing continued to fail. Baffled, we sat down with the operators to see what they were doing differently. In the Horizon UI, there's an option to launch multiple instances concurrently with a single API command. The operator's tenant had a quota of 100 instances, and they were specifying 100 instances when they went to test the platform. The first 8 would succeed, but the last 92 would fail. It turned out that the backend could only execute eight concurrent operations and anything more than that would error out. Our unit tests created multiple instances concurrently, but never more than eight, so we never caught the error.

There are a few different types of success scenarios that we need to plan for when architecting an OpenStack cloud.

First, we need to plan for a growth in the number of instances. This is relatively straightforward. Each additional instance grows the size of the database, it grows the amount of metering data in Ceilometer, and, most importantly, it will grow the number of compute nodes. Adding compute nodes and reporting puts strain on the message bus, which is typically the limiting factor in the size of OpenStack regions or cells. We'll talk more about this when we talk about dividing up OpenStack clouds into regions, cells, and availability zones.

The second type of growth we need to plan for is an increase in the number of API calls. Deployments which support **Continuous Integration(CI)** development environments might have (relatively) small compute requirements, but CI typically brings up and tears down environments rapidly. This will generate a large amount of API traffic, which in turn generates a large amount of database and message traffic.

In hosting environments, end users might also manually generate a lot of API traffic as they bring up and down instances, or manually check the status of deployments they've already launched. While a service catalog might check the status of instances it has launched on a regular basis, humans tend to hit **refresh** on their browsers in an erratic fashion. Automated testing of the platform has a tendency to grossly underestimate this kind of behavior.

With that in mind, any pattern that we adopt will need to provide for the following requirements:

- API services must continue to be available during a hardware failure in the control plane
- The systems which provide API services must be horizontally scalable (and ideally elastic) to respond to unanticipated demands
- The database services must be vertically or horizontally scalable to respond to unanticipated growth of the platform
- The message bus can either be vertically or horizontally scaled depending on the technology chosen

Finally, every system has its limits. These limits should be defined in the architecture documentation so that capacity planning can account for them. At some point, the control plane has scaled as far as it can and a second control plane should be deployed to provide additional capacity. Although OpenStack is designed to be massively scalable, it isn't designed to be infinitely scalable.

High availability patterns for the control plane

There are three approaches commonly used in OpenStack deployments these days for achieving high availability of the control plane.

The first is the simplest. Take the single-node cloud controller that we deployed in Chapter 2, *Architecting the Cloud*, virtualize it, and then make the virtual machine highly available using either VMware clustering or Linux clustering. While this option is simple and it provides for failure scenarios, it scales vertically (not horizontally) and doesn't provide for success scenarios. As such, it should only be used in regions with a limited number of compute nodes and a limited number of API calls. In practice, this method isn't used frequently and we won't spend any more time on it here.

The second pattern provides for H/A, but not horizontal scalability. This is the "Active/Passive" scenario described in the OpenStack High Availability Guide. At Red Hat, we used this a lot with our Folsom and Grizzly deployments, but moved away from it starting with Havana. It's similar to the virtualization solution described earlier but instead of relying on VMware clustering or Linux clustering to restart a failed virtual machine, it relies on Linux clustering to restart failed services on a second cloud controller node, also running the same subset of services. This pattern doesn't provide for success scenarios in the Web tier, but can still be used in the database and messaging tiers. Some networking services may still need to be provided as Active/Passive as well.

The third H/A pattern available to OpenStack architectures is the Active/Active pattern. In this pattern, services are horizontally scaled out behind a load balancing service or appliance, which is Active/Passive. As a general rule, most OpenStack services should be enabled as Active/Active where possible to allow for success scenarios while mitigating failure scenarios. Ideally, Active/Active services can be scaled out elastically without service disruption by simply adding additional control plane nodes.

Both of the Active/Passive and Active/Active designs require clustering software to determine the health of services and the hosts on which they run. In this chapter, we'll be using Pacemaker as the cluster manager. Some architects may choose to use Keepalived instead of Pacemaker.

In addition to these three scenarios, there are always limitations on scaling OpenStack services beyond a certain limit. As previously mentioned, the messaging bus is typically the first service to see issues with regard to scale; however, it's not the only place. During scale testing at Canonical and Mirantis, testers found issues with the Nova and Cinder projects as well as issues with the database service at scale. It is always best practice to monitor the responsiveness of all of the OpenStack services as well as performing scale testing using tools such as Tempest and/or Rally in a simulated environment to assess the impact of demand growth on your OpenStack clouds.

Active/Passive service configuration

In the Active/Passive service configuration, the service is configured and deployed to two or more physical systems. The service is associated with a **Virtual IP (VIP)**address. A cluster resource manager (normally Pacemaker) is used to ensure that the service and its VIP are enabled on only one of the two systems at any point in time. The resource manager may be configured to favor one of the machines over the other.

When the machine that the service is running on fails, the resource manager first ensures that the failed machine is no longer running and then it starts the service on the second machine. Ensuring that the failed machine is no longer running is accomplished through a process known as **fencing**. Fencing usually entails powering off the machine using the management interface on the BIOS. The fence agent may also talk to a power supply connected to the failed server to ensure that the system is down.

Some services (such as the Glance image registry) require shared storage to operate. If the storage is network-based, such as NFS, the storage may be mounted on both the active and the passive nodes simultaneously. If the storage is block-based, such as iSCSI, the storage will only be mounted on the active node and the resource manager will ensure that the storage migrates with the service and the VIP.

Active/Active service configuration

Most of the OpenStack API services are designed to be run on more than one system simultaneously. This configuration, the Active/Active configuration, requires a load balancer to spread traffic across each of the active services. The load balancer manages the VIP for the service and ensures that the backend systems are listening before forwarding traffic to them. The cluster manager ensures that the VIP is only active on one node at a time. The backend services may or may not be managed by the cluster manager in the Active/Active configuration. Service or system failure is detected by the load balancer and failed services are brought out of rotation.

There are a few different advantages to the Active/Active service configuration, which are as follows:

- The first advantage is that it allows for horizontal scalability. If additional capacity is needed for a given service, a new system can be brought up which is running the service and it can be added into rotation behind the load balancer without any downtime. The control plane may also be scaled down without downtime in the event that it was over-provisioned.
- The second advantage is that Active/Active services have a much shorter mean time to recovery. Fencing operations often take up to two minutes and fencing is required before the cluster resource manager will move a service from a failed system to a healthy one. Load balancers can immediately detect system failure and stop sending requests to unresponsive nodes while the cluster manager fences them in the background.

Whenever possible, architects should employ the Active/Active pattern for the control plane services.

OpenStack service specifics

In this section, we'll walk through each of the OpenStack services and outline the H/A strategy for them. While most of the services can be configured as Active/Active behind a load balancer, some of them must be configured as Active/Passive and others may be configured as Active/Passive. Some of the configuration is dependent on a particular version of OpenStack as well, especially, Ceilometer, Heat, and Neutron. The following details are current as of the Liberty release of OpenStack.

OpenStack web services

As a general rule, all of the web services and the Horizon dashboard may be run Active/Active. These include the API services for Keystone, Glance, Nova, Cinder, Neutron, Heat, and Ceilometer. The scheduling services for Nova, Cinder, Neutron, Heat, and Ceilometer may also be deployed Active/Active. These services do not require a load balancer, as they respond to requests on the message bus.

The only web service which must be run Active/Passive is the Ceilometer Central agent. This service can be configured to split its workload among multiple instances, however, to support scaling horizontally.

Database services

All state for the OpenStack web services is stored in a central database, usually a MySQL database. MySQL is usually deployed in an Active/Passive configuration, but can be made Active/Active with the Galera replication extension. Galera is clustering software for MySQL (MariaDB in OpenStack) and this uses synchronous replication to achieve H/A. However, even with Galera, we still recommend directing writes to only one of the replicas; some queries used by the OpenStack services may deadlock when writing to more than one master. With Galera, a load balancer is typically deployed in front of the cluster and is configured to deliver traffic to only one replica at a time. This configuration reduces the mean time to recovery of the service while ensuring that the data is consistent.

In practice, many organizations will defer to database architects for their preference regarding highly available MySQL deployments. After all, it is typically the database administration team who is responsible for responding to failures of that component.

Deployments which use the Ceilometer service also require a MongoDB database to store telemetry data. MongoDB is horizontally scalable by design and is typically deployed Active/Active with at least three replicas.

The message bus

All OpenStack services communicate through the message bus. Most OpenStack deployments these days use the RabbitMQ service as the message bus. RabbitMQ can be configured to be Active/Active through a facility known as "mirrored queues". The RabbitMQ service is not load- balanced; each service is given a list of potential nodes and the client is responsible for determining which nodes are active and which ones have failed.

Other messaging services used with OpenStack such as ZeroMQ, ActiveMQ, or Qpid may have different strategies and configurations for achieving H/A and horizontal scalability. For these services, refer to the documentation to determine the optimal architecture.

Compute, storage, and network agents

The compute, storage, and network components in OpenStack have a set of services, that perform the work which is scheduled by the API services. These services register themselves with the schedulers on start up over the message bus. The schedulers are responsible for determining the health of the services and scheduling work to active services. The compute and storage services are all designed to be run Active/Active but the network services need some extra consideration.

Each hypervisor in an OpenStack deployment runs the `nova-compute` service. When this service starts up, it registers itself with the `nova-scheduler` service. A list of currently available nova services is available via the `nova service-list` command. If a compute node is unavailable, its state is listed as down and the scheduler skips it when performing instance actions. When the node becomes available, the scheduler includes it in the list of available hosts.

For KVM or Xen-based deployments, the `nova-compute` service runs once per hypervisor and is not made highly available. For VMware-based deployments though, a single `nova-compute` service is run for every vSphere cluster. As such, this service should be made highly available in an Active/Passive configuration. This is typically done by virtualizing the service within a vSphere cluster and configuring the virtual machine to be highly available.

Cinder includes a service known as the `volume service` or `cinder-volume`. The volume service registers itself with the Cinder scheduler on startup and is responsible for creating, modifying, or deleting LUNs on block storage devices. For backends which support multiple writers, multiple copies of this service may be run in Active/Active configuration. The LVM backend (this is the reference backend) is not highly available, though, and may only have one cinder-volume service for each block device. This is because the LVM backend is responsible for providing iSCSI access to a locally attached storage device.

 For this reason, highly available deployments of OpenStack should avoid the LVM Cinder backend and instead use a backend that supports multiple `cinder-volume` services.

Finally, the Neutron component of OpenStack has a number of agents, which all require some special consideration for highly available deployments. The DHCP agent can be configured as highly available, and the number of agents which will respond to DHCP requests for each subnet is governed by a parameter in the `neutron.conf` file, `dhcp_agents_per_network`. This is typically set to 2, regardless of the number of DHCP agents which are configured to run in a control plane.

For most of the history of OpenStack, the L3 routing agent in Neutron has been a single point of failure. It could be made highly available in Active/Passive configuration, but its failover meant an interruption of network connections in the tenant space. Many of the third-party Neutron plugins have addressed this in different ways and the reference Open vSwitch plugin has a highly available L3 agent as of the Juno release. For details on implementing a solution to the single routing point of failure using OpenStack's **Distributed Virtual Routers** (DVR), refer to the OpenStack Foundation's Neutron documentation at `http://docs.openstack.org/liberty/networking-guide/scenario-dvr-ovs.html`.

Regions, cells, and availability zones

As we mentioned before, OpenStack is designed to be scalable, but not infinitely scalable. There are three different techniques architects can use to segregate an OpenStack cloud: regions, cells, and availability zones. In this section, we'll walk through how each of these concepts maps to hypervisor topologies.

Regions

From an end user's perspective, OpenStack regions are equivalent to regions in Amazon Web Services. Regions live in separate data centers and are often named after their geographical location. If your organization has a data center in Phoenix and one in Raleigh you'll have at least a PHX and a RDU region. Users who want to geographically disperse their workloads will place some of them in PHX and some of them in RDU. Regions have separate API endpoints, and although the Horizon UI has some support for multiple regions, they are essentially entirely separate deployments.

From an architectural standpoint, there are two main design choices for implementing regions, which are as follows:

- The first is around authorization. Users will want to have the same credentials for accessing each of the OpenStack regions. There are a few ways to accomplish this. The simplest way is to use a common backing store (usually LDAP) for the Keystone service in each region. In this scenario, the user has to authenticate separately to each region to get a token, but the credentials are the same.

 In Juno and later, Keystone also supports federation across regions. In this scenario, a Keystone token granted by one region can be presented to another region to authenticate a user. While this currently isn't widely used, it is a major focus area for the OpenStack Foundation and will probably see broader adoption in the future.

- The second major consideration for regional architectures is whether or not to present a single set of Glance images to each region. While work is currently being done to replicate Glance images across federated clouds, most organizations are manually ensuring that the shared images are consistent. This typically involves building a workflow around image publishing and deprecation which is mindful of the regional layout.

Another option for ensuring consistent images across regions is to implement a central image repository using Swift. This also requires shared Keystone and Glance services which span multiple data centers. Details on how to design multiple regions with shared services are in the OpenStack Architecture Design Guide.

Cells

The Nova compute service has the concept of cells, which can be used to segregate large pools of hypervisors within a single region. This technique is primarily used to mitigate the scalability limits of the OpenStack message bus. The deployment at CERN makes wide use of cells to achieve massive scalability within single regions.

Support for cells varies from service to service and as such cells are infrequently used outside a few very large cloud deployments. The CERN deployment is well-documented and should be used as a reference for these types of deployments.

In our experience, it's much simpler to deploy multiple regions within a single data center than to implement cells to achieve large scale. The added inconvenience of presenting your users with multiple API endpoints within a geographic location is typically outweighed by the benefits of having a more robust platform. If multiple control planes are available in a geographic region, the failure of a single control plane becomes less dramatic.

The cell architecture has its own set of challenges with regard to networking and scheduling of instance placement. Some very large companies that support the OpenStack effort have been working for years to overcome these hurdles. However, many different OpenStack distributions are currently working on a new control plane design. These new designs would begin to split the OpenStack control plane into containers running the OpenStack services in a microservice type architecture. This way the services themselves can be placed anywhere and be scaled horizontally based on the load. One architecture that has garnered a lot of attention lately is the Kolla project, which promotes Docker containers and Ansible playbooks to provide production-ready containers and deployment tools for operating OpenStack clouds. To see more, go to `https://wiki.openstack.org/wiki/Kolla`.

Availability zones

Availability zones are used to group hypervisors within a single OpenStack region. Availability zones are exposed to the end user and should be used to provide the user with an indication of the underlying topology of the cloud. The most common use case for availability zones is to expose failure zones to the user.

To ensure the H/A of a service deployed on OpenStack, a user will typically want to deploy the various components of their service onto hypervisors within different racks. This way, the failure of a top of rack switch or a PDU will only bring down a portion of the instances which provide the service. Racks form a natural boundary for availability zones for this reason. There are a few other interesting uses of availability zones apart from exposing failure zones to the end user. One financial services customer we work with had a requirement for the instances of each line of business to run on dedicated hardware. A combination of availability zones and the `AggregateMultiTenancyIsolation` Nova Scheduler filter was used to ensure that each tenant had access to dedicated compute nodes.

Availability zones can also be used to expose hardware classes to end users. For example, hosts with faster processors might be placed in one availability zone and hosts with slower processors might be placed in different availability zones. This allows end users to decide where to place their workloads based upon compute requirements.

Updating the design document

In this chapter, we walked through the different approaches and considerations for achieving H/A and scalability in OpenStack deployments. As Cloud Architects, we need to decide on the correct approach for our deployment and then document it thoroughly so that it can be evaluated by the larger team in our organization.

Each of the major OpenStack vendors has a reference architecture for highly available deployments and these should be used as a starting point for the design. The design should then be integrated with the existing Enterprise Architecture and modified to ensure that best practices established by the various stakeholders within an organization are followed.

For example, Red Hat's highly available control plane uses the Galera extension to achieve Active/Active MariaDB services, but the database architects within an organization may only support Oracle's MySQL in an Active/Passive configuration. The Cloud Architect may choose to implement the database architect's proven pattern instead if they intend on asking for support from the database administration team. The network architects within an organization may be more comfortable supporting *F5* load balancers than HAProxy load balancers.

The system administrators within an organization may be more comfortable supporting Pacemaker than `Keepalived`. The design document presents the choices made for each of these key technologies and gives the stakeholders an opportunity to comment on them before the deployment.

Planning the physical architecture

In the previous chapter, we updated the *Physical architecture* section to include a definition of the various host groups which we will be deploying. The simplest way to achieve H/A is to add additional cloud controllers to the deployment and cluster them. Other deployments may choose to segregate services into different host classes, which can then be clustered. This may include separating the database services into database nodes, separating the messaging services into messaging nodes, and separating the `memcached` service into memcache nodes.

Load balancing services might live on their own nodes as well. The primary considerations for mapping scalable services to physical (or virtual) hosts are the following:

- Does the service scale horizontally or vertically?
- Will vertically scaling the service impede the performance of other co-located services?
- Does the service have particular hardware or network requirements that other services don't have?

For example, some OpenStack deployments which use the HAProxy load balancing service chose to separate out the load balancing nodes on a separate hardware. The VIPs which the load balancing nodes host must live on a public, routed network, while the internal IPs of services that they route to don't have that requirement. Putting the HAProxy service on separate hosts allows the rest of the control plane to only have private addressing.

Grouping all of the API services on dedicated hosts may ease horizontal scalability. These services don't need to be managed by a cluster resource manager and can be scaled by adding additional nodes to the load balancers without having to update cluster definitions. Database services have high I/O requirements. Segregating these services onto machines which have access to a high-performance fibre channel may make sense.

Finally, you should consider whether or not to virtualize the control plane. If the control plane will be virtualized, creating additional host groups to host dedicated services becomes very attractive. Having eight or nine virtual machines dedicated to the control plane is a very different proposition from having eight or nine physical machines dedicated to the control plane.

Most highly available control planes require at least three nodes to ensure that quorum is easily determined by the cluster resource manager. While dedicating three physical nodes to the control function of a hundred node OpenStack deployment makes a lot of sense, dedicating nine physical nodes may not. Many of the organizations that we've worked with will already have a VMware-based cluster available for hosting management appliances and the control plane can be deployed within that existing footprint. Organizations which are deploying a KVM-only cloud may not want to incur the additional operational complexity of managing the additional virtual machines outside OpenStack.

Updating the physical architecture design

Once the mapping of services to physical (or virtual) machines has been determined, the design document should be updated to include a definition of the host groups and their associated functions. A simple example is provided as follows:

- **Load balancer**: These systems provide the load balancing services in an Active/Passive configuration
- **Cloud controller**: These systems provide the API services, the scheduling services, and the Horizon dashboard services in an Active/Active configuration
- **Database node**: These systems provide the MySQL database services in an Active/Passive configuration
- **Messaging node**: These systems provide the RabbitMQ messaging services in an Active/Active configuration
- **Compute node**: These systems act as KVM hypervisors and run the `nova-compute` and `openvswitch-agent` services

Deployments which will be using only the cloud controller host group might use the following definitions:

- **Cloud controller**: These systems provide the load balancing services in an Active/Passive configuration and the API services, MySQL database services, and RabbitMQ messaging services in an Active/Active configuration
- **Compute node**: These systems act as KVM hypervisors and run the nova-compute and openvswitch-agent services

After defining the host groups, the physical architecture diagram should be updated to reflect the mapping of host groups to physical machines in the deployment. This should also include considerations for network connectivity. The following is an example architecture diagram for inclusion in the design document:

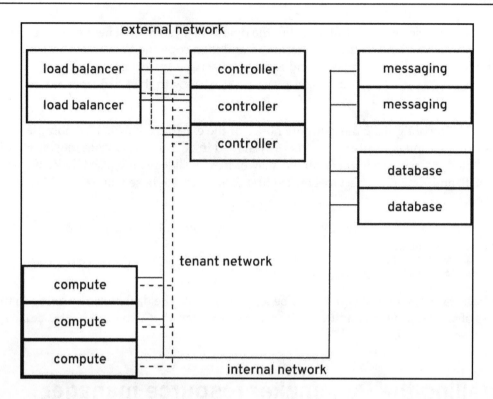

Implementing H/A in the lab deployment

In this last section, we'll make the current lab deployment that we deployed in Chapter 2, *Architecting the Cloud*, highly available by adding a second controller node and configuring cluster software. This example should be simple enough to easily implement in the lab while still allowing you to evaluate the technology.

Provisioning a second controller

In later chapters we'll look at more flexible deployment methodologies that allow fine-grained service placement and automated cluster configuration. In this chapter, we'll just extend the Packstack deployment from Chapter 2, *Architecting the Cloud*. Packstack isn't designed to deploy multiple controllers, so some manual configuration of services will be required.

To provision the second controller, install the operating system on a new machine in the same way you provisioned the first controller and then copy the Packstack answer file from the first controller. Edit the answer and replace CONFIG_CONTROLLER_HOST, CONFIG_NETWORK_HOSTS, and CONFIG_STORAGE_HOST with the IP address of the new controller.

We won't be reconfiguring the compute nodes or the existing controller, so add the compute nodes and controller that you provisioned in Chapter 2, *Architecting the Cloud*, to the EXCLUDE_SERVERS parameter in the answer file. We'll leave the MySQL, Redis, MongoDB, and RabbitMQ services on the first controller, so those values should not be modified.

Run Packstack on the new controller using the same command we used in Chapter 2, *Architecting the Cloud*:

```
packstack --answer-file <answer-file>
```

After Packstack completes, you should be able to log in to the dashboard by going to the IP address of the second host and using the same credentials that you used in Chapter 2, *Architecting the Cloud*.

Installing the Pacemaker resource manager

Next, we'll install Pacemaker to manage the VIPs that we'll use with HAProxy to make the web services highly available. We assume that the cluster software is already available via yum to the controller nodes.

1. First, install Pacemaker on both nodes using the following command:

   ```
   # yum install -y pcs fence-agents-all
   ```

2. Verify that the software installed correctly by running the following command:

   ```
   # rpm -q pcs
   pcs-0.9.137-13.el7_1.3.x86_64
   ```

3. Next, add rules to the firewall to allow cluster traffic:

   ```
   # firewall-cmd --permanent --add-service=high-availability
   ```

4. Set the password for the Pacemaker cluster on each node using the following command:

```
# passwd hacluster
```

5. Start the Pacemaker cluster manager on each node:

```
# systemctl start pcsd.service
# systemctl enable pcsd.service
```

6. Then, authenticate the nodes using the following commands on the first node:

```
# pcs cluster auth controller1 controller2
Username: hacluster
Password:
controller1: Authorized
controller2: Authorized
```

7. Finally, run the following commands on the first node to create the cluster and start it:

```
# pcs cluster setup --start --name openstack \
> controller1 controller2
Shutting down pacemaker/corosync services...
Redirecting to /bin/systemctl stop  pacemaker.service
Redirecting to /bin/systemctl stop  corosync.service
Killing any remaining services...
Removing all cluster configuration files...
controller1: Succeeded
controller2: Succeeded
Starting cluster on nodes: controller1, controller2...
controller1: Starting Cluster...
controller2: Starting Cluster...
```

8. For our example cluster, we will disable fencing using the following command:

```
# pcs property set stonith-enabled=false
```

9. Verify that the cluster started successfully using the following command:

```
# pcs status
Cluster name: openstack
Last updated: Mon Aug 31 01:51:47 2015
Last change: Mon Aug 31 01:51:14 2015
Stack: corosync
Current DC: controller1 (1) - partition with quorum
Version: 1.1.12-a14efad
2 Nodes configured
0 Resources configured
Online: [ controller1 controller2 ]
```

 For more information on setting up Pacemaker, see the excellent Clusters from Scratch documentation at http://clusterlabs.org/doc/en-US/Pac emaker/1.1-pcs/html/Clusters_from_Scratch/index.html.

Installing and configuring HAProxy

We'll be using HAProxy to load-balance our control plane services in this lab deployment. Some deployments may also implement Keepalived and run HAProxy in an Active/Active configuration. For this deployment, we'll run HAProxy Active/Passive and manage it as a resource along with our VIP in Pacemaker.

To start, install HAProxy on both nodes using the following command:

```
# yum -y install haproxy
```

Verify installation with the following command:

```
# rpm -q haproxy
haproxy-1.5.4-4.el7_1.x86_64
```

Next, we will create a configuration file for HAProxy which load-balances the API services installed on the two controllers. Use the following example as a template, replacing the IP addresses in the example with the IP addresses of the two controllers and the IP address of the VIP that you'll be using to load-balance the API services.

Some deployments may chose to create a VIP for each service. This allows multiple HAProxy nodes to answer HTTP sessions for different services. In this example, we'll only use a single VIP since HAProxy is in Active/Passive configuration.

The following example `/etc/haproxy/haproxy.cfg`, will load-balance Horizon in our environment:

```
global
   daemon
   group  haproxy
   maxconn  40000
   pidfile  /var/run/haproxy.pid
   user  haproxy

defaults
   log  127.0.0.1 local2 warning
   mode  tcp
   option  tcplog
   option  redispatch
   retries  3
   timeout  connect 10s
   timeout  client 60s
   timeout  server 60s
   timeout  check 10s

listen horizon
   bind 192.168.0.30:80
   mode http
   cookie SERVERID insert indirect nocache
   option tcplog
   timeout client 180s
   server controller1 192.168.0.10:80 cookie controller1 check inter 1s
   server controller2 192.168.0.11:80 cookie controller2 check inter 1s
```

In this example, `controller1` has an IP address of `192.168.0.10` and `controller2` has an IP address of `192.168.0.11`. The VIP that we've chosen to use is `192.168.0.30`. Copy this file, replacing the IP addresses with the addresses in your lab, to `/etc/haproxy/haproxy.cfg` on each of the controllers.

In order for Horizon to respond to requests on the VIP, we'll need to add the VIP as a ServerAlias in the Apache virtual host configuration. This is found at `/etc/httpd/conf.d/15-horizon_vhost.conf` in our lab installation. Look for the following line:

```
ServerAlias 192.168.0.10
```

Add an additional `ServerAlias` line with the VIP on both controllers:

```
ServerAlias 192.168.0.30
```

You'll also need to tell Apache not to listen on the VIP so that HAProxy can bind to the address. To do this, modify `/etc/httpd/conf/ports.conf` and specify the IP address of the controller in addition to the port numbers. The following is an example:

```
Listen 192.168.0.10:35357
Listen 192.168.0.10:5000
Listen 192.168.0.10:80
```

In this example, `192.168.0.10` is the address of the first controller. Substitute the appropriate IP address for each machine.

Restart Apache to pick up the new alias:

```
# systemctl restart httpd.service
```

Next, add the VIP and the HAProxy service to the Pacemaker cluster as resources. These commands should only be run on the first node:

```
# pcs resource create VirtualIP IPaddr2 ip=192.168.0.30 cidr_netmask=24
# pcs resource create HAProxy systemd:haproxy
```

Co-locate the HAProxy service with the VirtualIP to ensure that the two run together:

```
# pcs constraint colocation add VirtualIP with HAProxy score=INFINITY
```

Verify that the resources have been started:

```
# pcs status
...
Full list of resources:
VirtualIP (ocf::heartbeat:IPaddr2):Started controller1
HAProxy (systemd:haproxy):Started controller1
...
```

At this point, you should be able to access Horizon using the VIP you specified. Traffic will flow from your client to HAProxy on the VIP to Apache on one of the two nodes.

Additional API service configuration

Now that we have a working cluster and HAProxy configuration, the final configuration step is to move each of the OpenStack API endpoints behind the load balancer. There are three steps in this process, which are as follows:

1. Update the HAProxy configuration to include the service.
2. Move the endpoint in the Keystone service catalog to the VIP.
3. Reconfigure services to point to the VIP instead of the IP of the first controller.

In the following example, we will move the Keystone service behind the load balancer. This process can be followed for each of the API services.

First, add a section to the HAProxy configuration file for the authorization and admin endpoints of Keystone:

```
listen keystone-admin
  bind 192.168.0.30:35357
  mode tcp
  option tcplog
  server controller1 192.168.0.10:35357 check inter 1s
  server controller2 192.168.0.11:35357 check inter 1s

listen keystone-public
  bind 192.168.0.30:5000
  mode tcp
  option tcplog
  server controller1 192.168.0.10:5000 check inter 1s
  server controller2 192.168.0.11:5000 check inter 1s
```

Make sure to update the configuration on both of the controllers. Restart the haproxy service on the active node:

```
# systemctl restart haproxy.service
```

You can determine the active node with the output from pcs status. Check to make sure that HAProxy is now listening on ports 5000 and 35357 using the following commands:

```
# curl http://192.168.0.30:5000
# curl http://192.168.0.30:35357
```

Both should output some JSON describing the status of the Keystone service.

Next, update the endpoint for the identity service in the Keystone service catalog by creating a new endpoint and deleting the old one:

```
# . ./keystonerc_admin
# openstack endpoint list
+-------------------------------+------------+---------------+---------
------+
| ID                            | Region     | Service Name  | Service
Type |
+-------------------------------+------------+---------------+---------
------+
| 14f32353dd7d497d9816bf0302279d23 | RegionOne | keystone     |
identity      |
. . .
# openstack endpoint create \
--adminurl http://192.168.0.30:35357/v2.0 \
--internalurl http://192.168.0.30:5000/v2.0 \
--publicurl http://192.168.0.30:5000/v2.0 \
--region RegionOne keystone
+--------------+-------------------------------------+
| Field        | Value                               |
+--------------+-------------------------------------+
| adminurl     | http://192.168.0.30:35357/v2.0      |
| id           | c590765ca1a847db8b79aa5f40cd2110 |
. . .
# openstack endpoint delete 14f32353dd7d497d9816bf0302279d23
```

Last, update the auth_uri and identity_uri parameters in each of the OpenStack services to point to the new IP address. The following configuration files will need to be edited:

- /etc/ceilometer/ceilometer.conf
- /etc/cinder/api-paste.ini
- /etc/glance/glance-api.conf
- /etc/glance/glance-registry.conf
- /etc/neutron/neutron.conf
- /etc/neutron/api-paste.ini
- /etc/nova/nova.conf
- /etc/swift/proxy-server.conf

After editing each of the files, restart the OpenStack services on all of the nodes in the lab deployment using the following command:

```
# openstack-service restart
```

The OpenStack services will now be using the Keystone API endpoint provided by the VIP and the service will be highly available. The architecture used in this cluster is relatively simple, but it provides an example of both Active/Active and Active/Passive service configurations.

Summary

A complete guide to implementing H/A of the OpenStack services is probably worth a book to itself. In this chapter we started out by covering the main strategies for making OpenStack services highly available and identifying which strategies apply well to each service. Then we covered how OpenStack deployments are typically segmented across physical regions. Finally, we updated our documentation and implemented a few of the technologies we discussed in the lab.

While walking through the main considerations for highly available deployments in this chapter, we've tried to emphasize a few key points:

- Scalability is at least as important as H/A in cluster design.
- Ensure that your design is flexible in case of unexpected growth.
- OpenStack doesn't scale forever. Plan for multiple regions.

Also, it's important to make sure that the strategy and architecture that you adopt for H/A are supportable by your organization. Consider reusing existing architectures for H/A in the message bus and database layers.

References

- The OpenStack High Availability Guide: `http://docs.openstack.org/high-av ailability-guide`
- The OpenStack Architecture Design Guide: `http://docs.openstack.org/arch- design/content/index.html`
- Clusters from Scratch: `http://clusterlabs.org/doc/en-US/Pacemaker/1.1/ht ml/Clusters_from_Scratch/`

4
Building the Deployment Pipeline

We often tell customers we work with that OpenStack is not **installed**, it is **deployed**. While the difference in words might seem subtle, it can really be a revolutionary change within an organization. Most enterprise infrastructure teams are used to the following process in the deployment of a new infrastructure platform:

1. Install the platform.
2. Configure and integrate the platform.
3. Run the platform.
4. Upgrade the platform.

Installing and configuring the platform can take months or years and once it's installed, the platform is expected to run for years. Upgrades to the platform happen every 3 to 5 years and are large 6-12 month projects. Red Hat has structured the release of our Enterprise Linux operating system around these cycles – there were 3 years between the release of RHEL 5 and RHEL 6 and almost 4 years between RHEL 6 and RHEL 7. Each release is supported for 10 years and conservative infrastructure teams will wait at least a year after the release of a new version to start their 6-12 month upgrade project.

This kind of conservative approach to platform deployment has worked extremely well in the operating system, virtualization platform, and application platform space. However, if the most important business driver for your private cloud project is increased agility, you are unlikely to achieve your goal with a 12 month roll-out and a 5 year life cycle.

In this chapter, we'll be looking at how OpenStack is typically deployed as application software, not as infrastructure software. We'll build a simple deployment pipeline which uses Puppet to describe an OpenStack deployment, uses Jenkins an open source **Continuous Integration** (**CI**) tool to realize that deployment, and then runs unit tests to verify that the deployment meets our specifications. Throughout the chapter, we'll talk about iterative development and how it applies to OpenStack deployments.

Dealing with Infrastructure as a Software

A Vice President of Infrastructure at a large company once told us something like this, "I like hardware. My hardware hardly ever breaks. The software I deploy breaks all the time. When my data center becomes software, how will I ever have a stable platform?". While the same concern could (and probably should) have once been applied to virtualization, most organizations today are very comfortable with the idea of software pretending to be hardware. The software-defined data center is something a little more intimidating, though. While we've had software pretend to be a CPU for a long time, we've only had software pretend to be a storage array relatively recently. Also, when the storage array goes down, everything tends to come down with it.

However, maybe the bigger question is around software constantly breaking on deployment. Indeed, the most successful OpenStack deployments that we've worked with have all adopted modern software development techniques to ensure that their software does not break on deployment.

Eating the elephant

The first and most important concept that we will apply to our deployment process is that of iterative development. Instead of trying to tackle all of the requirements that we've identified in one deployment, we break it down into stories, assign them to two or three week sprints, and then implement them one by one. A sprint is a basic measure of development derived from the Scrum process and framework. A sprint is a timeboxed measure of effort that is planned and limited to a specific duration (two weeks is common). Not only does this allow us to limit the complexity of each release and focus on thoroughly testing each component, it also allows us to begin returning value to the business much sooner in the process. Workloads that only require a small feature set will be able to board the platform without waiting for a large release.

Writing the tests first

The second most important practice that we will pull from the software development world is that of test-driven development. We write the test that demonstrates the functionality we're implementing first and then work on the deployment until the test passes. Once the feature has been implemented, the test then becomes part of the routine monitoring system for the platform.

In our experience, if the tests aren't written before the code, they are frequently not written. Every project runs out of time at some point and if the tests are the last thing on the list, they tend to get cut.

Always be deploying

The benefits of continuous deployment have been well described for some time in the software development world, but they're particularly applicable to OpenStack deployments. Lots of small, well-tested changes tend to cause much less disruption to a complex environment such as a private cloud deployment than a few, huge well-tested changes.

There are some exceptions to this, though. For example, moving from Nova Networking to Neutron is a major change that cannot easily be broken up into smaller pieces. Adding a new Cinder driver is a small iterative change, but changing from one Cinder driver to another can be a massive change in environments with large numbers of volumes to migrate. Care should be taken when making architectural decisions to try to avoid large changes to the platform that cannot be iteratively developed and deployed.

Using configuration management for deployment

The first tool required to begin deploying our platform-like code is to introduce a configuration management system. While it is certainly possible to automate the deployment of OpenStack using shell scripts (we've seen it done), using a declarative configuration management tool makes it much more simple for your team to track changes between iterations. Also, an OpenStack configuration can contain hundreds of variables that need to be set across several configuration files on dozens of hosts. For example, our lab deployment of Kilo has 137 parameters set in the composition layer. Managing this level of complexity with shell scripts introduces another unnecessary level of complexity.

Every OpenStack user survey for the past couple of years has asked the community how they typically deploy OpenStack. While a wide variety of methods are represented in the results, the clear leader has been Puppet for some time now. A new initiative in the community has grown up around Ansible in the last year and its use has increased dramatically. A few prominent OpenStack users also use Chef for deployment. Our recommendation is to use the tool that your organization has the most experience with. Some of the groups that we've worked with already had large implementations of Puppet, some of them had expertise in Chef, and some prefer to use Ansible. We've also worked on projects which leveraged Salt. A new trend that is emerging is to use a combination of tools. You might have Ansible or Salt initiate Puppet runs on your hosts, for example. Puppet is most frequently used and we'll use it in the examples in this chapter.

Using the community modules

Each of the configuration management systems referenced earlier has a set of modules for deploying OpenStack that are written and maintained by the OpenStack community. For example, consider the following table:

Orchestration tool's OpenStack modules	Location
Puppet modules	`https://wiki.openstack.org/wiki/Puppet`
Ansible playbooks	`https://wiki.openstack.org/wiki/OpenStackAnsible`
Chef cookbooks	`https://wiki.openstack.org/wiki/Chef`

Regardless of the technology used, the overall approach is the same.

A deployment starts with the creation of what we'll refer to as the **composition layer**. This is a Puppet module (or Ansible playbook or Chef cookbook) which defines the roles that we want the systems in our deployment to take in terms of the community modules. For example, we might define a compute role as a class which would include the `nova::compute` class. The controller role would include the `keystone`, `glance`, `nova::api`, and other classes. We may also pull in other Puppet modules to configure system services such as NTP or to install monitoring agents.

Assigning roles

Once we've declared our roles in the composition layer, we need a mechanism via which we apply them to systems. The tool that we've been using up to this point (Packstack) does this over SSH – it generates a set of puppet manifests which include the community modules and then it applies them to the systems in our lab one by one. It supports two roles: the controller role and the compute role. Our lab deployment currently has controller and compute nodes, but we'll also be defining database nodes which can run the database and messaging services.

Many of the organizations that we've worked with have used Cobbler (`http://cobbler.github.io`), Foreman (`http://theforeman.org`), Puppet Enterprise (`https://puppetlabs.com/puppet/puppet-enterprise`), or some other tool to assign roles to systems. These tools are referred to as **External Node Classifiers** (**ENC**) for Puppet. With an ENC it's easy to separate the configuration parameters, such as IP addresses or passwords, from the configuration itself in the system. These tools can also provide reporting on Puppet runs and management functionality.

In this chapter, we'll set up a simple Puppet master which will manage the configuration of the hosts in our environment. We'll store configuration data in our composition layer, acknowledging that it's not a best practice.

 There is one customer we've worked with who preferred to store configuration data in the composition layer. Their reasoning was that inputting the configuration data was the most common place for a typo or other mistake that would wreck an automated deployment. Since they were tracking the data in version control, it was easier to track these manual errors. The process that they came up with was to fork a branch for each environment that they deployed and then pull configuration changes down to the branches from the master as they needed to update them. Forking typically happens when developers take a copy of source code from a project such as OpenStack and start adding their own changes. Since the main source code for a project is called the trunk, when a developer changes a part of the code, it is said that the developer has created a branch.

We'll assign the roles we've defined to the hosts on the Puppet master and when hosts check in with the master, they'll be given the configuration which matches their role. Hosts check in periodically after the first run and will pull updates to the configuration as we make them available on the master.

Choosing a starting point

Each of the official OpenStack Puppet, Chef, and Ansible projects listed earlier provide example composition layers which will do a simple all-in-one deployment. The Puppet all-in-one deployment manifest is available at `https://github.com/openstack/puppet-openstack-integration`. It provides three scenarios, which can be used as a starting point. Different OpenStack vendors may also have references which make good starting points. Some organizations we've worked with have hired consulting firms to write their initial composition layer and then teach them how to iterate on it.

Since we already have a working deployment using Packstack, we'll use that as a basis for our composition layer. As we add features to our deployment, we'll copy in pieces from the manifests generated by Packstack as a starting point. We'll also add some new Puppet code to extend the deployment beyond what's possible with Packstack.

Test infrastructure

Regardless of the configuration management system that your organization decides to use to deploy and configure the OpenStack software, it is critical that the deployment process is driven by the test infrastructure. It has been our experience that manually administrated environments always result in inconsistency, regardless of the skill of the operator performing the deployment. Automated deployments cannot happen in a vacuum; however, for them to be successful they need to provide immediate feedback to the developer and operator so that they can decide whether or not the deployment was successful. We've been through a lot of manual deployments and manual acceptance tests of OpenStack and the cycles can take days or weeks to complete.

Types of testing

There are several stages of testing that are applied to the changes in the composition layer before they're applied to the environment. At each stage, the deployment is stopped if the tests fail. We refer to this set of stages as the **deployment pipeline**. Changes are committed to version control on one end of the pipeline and the configuration is realized in the infrastructure on the other end.

The following table lists the items which are tested at each stage in the pipeline:

Stage	Test focus
Pre-commit	Before the change enters the pipeline, it is tested to ensure that there are no syntax errors or style issues.
Deployment testing	At this stage, each of the systems in the test cluster attempts to apply the configuration update. Success is indicated by whether or not the change is applied without errors. Some deployments will initiate a second application to test for idempotency.
Integration testing	Once the test cluster has successfully applied the configuration, a unit test suite is run against the OpenStack APIs, verifying the functionality of the configuration.
Performance testing	A series of tests are run against the test cluster to ensure that the change did not adversely affect performance.
Acceptance testing	At this stage in the pipeline, any manual testing is performed. The change is then promoted to the next environment.
Canary testing	A subset of the production environment is updated with the change and automated and the acceptance testing is repeated with the production database and hypervisors.
Release	The entire production environment is updated with the change.

Many organizations will want to include a code review in the deployment process. This is typically done after all automated testing is complete so that the results are available to the reviewer. Tools such as Gerrit (https://www.gerritcodereview.com/) are available to orchestrate build pipelines which have code review requirements. Many organizations will prefer to perform canary testing and production releases manually – these should still be automated processes which are initiated (and rolled back) at the discretion of operators.

Writing the tests

OpenStack is entirely driven by the REST API and it is possible to write tests for the platform in any language which has a HTTP client implementation. There are software development kits available at `http://developer.openstack.org` for most of the popular languages. That said, most organizations tend to write their tests in Python (the language OpenStack is written in). There are two schools of thought on this. The first is that it is easier to attract OpenStack talent who know Python and the skill is transferable between testing and development. Also, there is an upstream Python project called **Tempest**, which many organizations use as a framework for running their own tests. The second school of thought is that organizations should test the platform using the same interface that end users of the platform will use. For example, if your intention is for the infrastructure to be provisioned from a Cloud Management Platform or a PaaS using the `Ruby Fog` library (`http://fog.io/`), then your tests should be written using the Fog library.

Either way, Tempest is almost always used in some part of the testing process for OpenStack deployments. If nothing else, all public clouds which advertise themselves as OpenStack clouds must pass a minimum set of Tempest tests to achieve certification with the Foundation.

Running the tests

As we mentioned earlier, the test infrastructure should drive the changes through the pipeline, capturing the results of each test run and promoting changes when the runs are successful. Any of the many CI tools used for software development can be used for this purpose. What we typically recommend is to leverage the CI tools and software repositories that your organization is already using. If your organization isn't doing CI in your software development group, good choices that we've seen used successfully before are Jenkins (`https://jenkins-ci.org/`), Atlassian's Bamboo (`https://www.atlassian.com/software/bamboo/`), or Buildbot (`http://buildbot.net/`). The OpenStack Foundation's CI is built around Jenkins and that's the tool that we'll use in this chapter to build our pipeline.

Putting the pipeline together

Now that we've described the different components of the deployment pipeline, let's assemble an example pipeline in our lab environment. We'll start by setting up the CI server, creating a new composition layer, writing a unit test, and then deploying the OpenStack infrastructure to pass the test.

Setting up the CI server

In previous chapters, we deployed OpenStack by running the `packstack` utility from the cloud controller. In this section, we'll be setting up a dedicated machine to do our deployments. The requirements for our deployment machine are not too strenuous – any machine running CentOS 7 with 2 GB of RAM or more should suffice. The only network requirements are that the machine is reachable from both the intranet and from the OpenStack cluster itself.

Installing Git

The following instructions will set up a Git version control server on the CI server. If you already have access to a Git repository or prefer to use GitHub you can skip this section. For more information on setting up a Git server, refer to the *Pro Git* book by *Scott Chacon* and *Ben Straub*, available on the Internet at `https://git-scm.com/book/en/v2/`.

To install the Apache HTTP server and the Git version control software, execute the following steps:

1. Execute the following command as root on the CI server:

   ```
   # yum install -y httpd git
   ```

2. Verify that the packages were correctly installed:

   ```
   # rpm -q httpd git
   ```

3. Create a top-level directory to hold our repository:

   ```
   # mkdir /var/www/html/git
   ```

4. Create the Git repository in the directory with the following commands:

   ```
   # mkdir /var/www/html/git/openstack/
   # cd /var/www/html/git/openstack
   # git --bare init
   # git update-server-info
   ```

5. You should see the following response after the `git --bare init` command:

   ```
   Initialized empty Git repository in
   /var/www/git/openstack/
   ```

6. Reset permissions on the new Git repository for Apache:

```
# chown -R apache:apache /var/www/html/git/
```

7. Finally, create a configuration file which requires authentication for the Git repository. The following example can be copied to `/etc/httpd/conf.d/git.conf`:

```
<Directory /var/www/html/git/>
  DAV on

  AuthName "Git login:"
  AuthType Basic
  AuthUserFile /var/www/htpasswd

  # Allow anonymous clone, but require auth for push.
  <LimitExcept GET PROPFIND>
    Require valid-user
  </LimitExcept>
</Directory>
```

8. Create a user account for us to use for the repository:

```
# htpasswd -c /var/www/htpasswd git
```

9. Last, restart the `httpd` server:

```
# systemctl restart httpd
```

10. You should now be able to clone the Git repository using the following command:

```
# git clone http://git@localhost/git/openstack
```

11. You may be prompted for the password that you entered when creating the user account and you should receive the following message:

```
warning: You appear to have cloned an empty
repository.
```

Installing a Puppet master

The following instructions will set up a Puppet master on the CI server. If you already have a Puppet infrastructure that you can use in your lab, you can skip this section. For more information on setting up a Puppet master, refer to the Puppet Reference Manual (http://d ocs.puppetlabs.com/puppet/latest/reference/). Install the RDO repository, which provides access to both the Puppet and the OpenStack Puppet modules using the following steps:

1. Execute the following command as root on the CI server:

   ```
   # yum install -y https://rdoproject.org/repos/rdo-release.rpm
   ```

2. Verify that the repository has been enabled by running the following command:

   ```
   # yum repolist
   ```

3. You should see the openstack repository in the output. Run the following command to install Puppet and the OpenStack Puppet modules:

   ```
   # yum install -y puppet puppet-server openstack-puppet-modules
   openstack-packstack
   ```

4. Verify their installation with the following command:

   ```
   # rpm -q puppet puppet-server openstack-puppet-modules
   openstack-packstack
   ```

5. Edit the puppet configuration to include the OpenStack Puppet modules:

   ```
   # puppet config set basemodulepath \
   '$confdir/modules:/usr/share/puppet/modules:/usr/share/openstack\
   -puppet/modules' --section main
   ```

6. Verify the configuration by listing the available Puppet modules:

   ```
   # puppet module list
   ```

   You should see around 60 Puppet modules, depending on the version of OpenStack. Ignore any errors about dependencies.

7. Start the `puppet master` service using the following command:

```
# systemctl start puppetmaster.service
# systemctl enable puppetmaster.service
```

8. Verify that the service started correctly:

```
# systemctl status puppetmaster.server -l
```

You should see that the service has created a certificate authority. It is important that the clients in your environment access the Puppet master using the same hostname as the certificate authority. If the clients will be accessing the Puppet master over more than the hostname, look into using the `dns_alt_names` setting for `puppet.conf`.

Installing Jenkins

The following instructions will set up a Jenkins server on the CI server. If you already have a Jenkins server that you can use in your lab, you can skip this section. For more information on setting up Jenkins, refer to the Jenkins website (`https://wiki.jenkins-ci.org/display/JENKINS/Use+Jenkins`).

1. Execute the following commands as root on the CI server to install the Jenkins repository, which provides access to Jenkins:

```
# curl http://pkg.jenkins-ci.org/redhat/jenkins.repo >
/etc/yum.repos.d/jenkins.repo
# rpm --import https://jenkins-ci.org/redhat/jenkins-ci.org.key
# yum install -y java-1.7.0-openjdk jenkins
```

2. To verify that the software was installed correctly, run the following command:

```
# rpm -q java-1.7.0-openjdk jenkins
```

3. To start the `jenkins` server, use the following command:

```
# systemctl start jenkins
```

4. Verify that Jenkins started correctly using the following command:

```
# systemctl status jenkins -l
```

You should see that the service is running and that there are no errors in the log output.

5. You can now log in to the Jenkins web UI by visiting your host on port `8080` in your web browser; that is, if your CI server's hostname is `jenkins.example.com`, Jenkins should be available at `http://jenkins.example.com:8080/`. You should see the following page upon login:

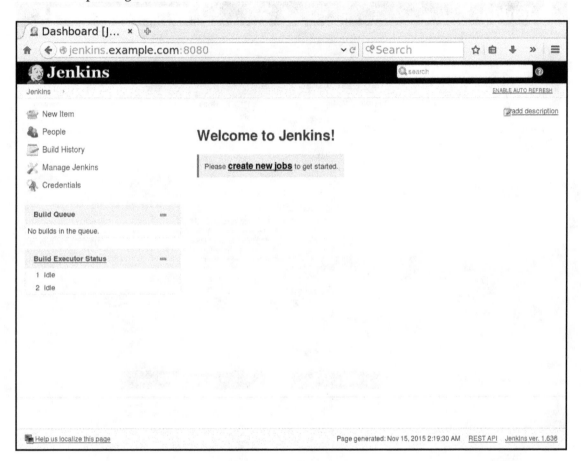

6. The last thing we'll need to do is install the Git SCM plugin. Click on the **Manage Jenkins** link in the left-hand navigation. Select **Manage Plugins** from the next page. On the **Plugins** page, select the **Available** tab and search for `git plugin` in the **Filter** bar. Select the **Git** plugin and click on **Install without restart**:

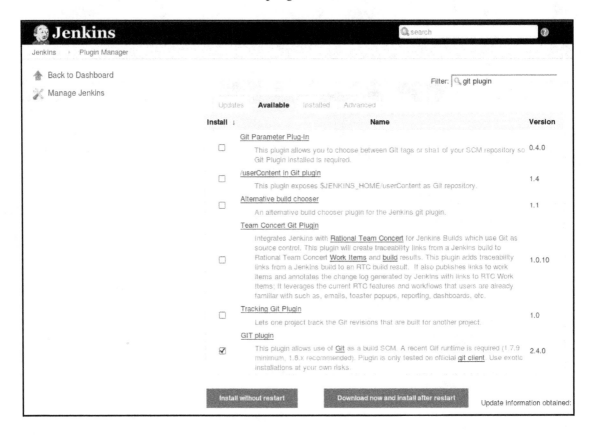

You'll see the status of the installation as it progresses. When it completes successfully, you'll see a page similar to this:

Jenkins is now installed and configured with the Git Plugin.

Creating the composition layer

Now that our infrastructure software is in place, we'll begin creating our composition layer. As we mentioned earlier, we'll be starting with the "known good" configuration we got from running the `packstack` command in `Chapter 2`, *Architecting the Cloud*.

Starting our Puppet modules

Our composition layer will be stored in two Puppet modules, using the **profiles and roles** pattern developed by Craig Dunn (http://www.craigdunn.org/2012/05/239/). We'll store the modules in a directory called puppet/modules in our new Git repository. The following steps will create the new modules within our repository:

1. Clone the repository. It is recommended to use an unprivileged user account for this section:

    ```
    $ git clone http://git@localhost/git/openstack/
    ```

2. Next, create the directory for the modules:

    ```
    $ mkdir -p openstack/puppet/modules
    ```

3. Use the puppet module command to create the new modules in the directory:

    ```
    $ cd openstack/puppet/modules
    $ puppet module generate openstack-profile
    $ puppet module generate openstack-role
    ```

    For each of these commands, you will be prompted for a set of metadata about the module. Enter as much information as you'd like or take the defaults.

4. Once you've set up the modules as you like, go back to the top level of the code repository and check them into revision control with the following commands:

    ```
    $ cd ~/openstack
    $ git add puppet
    $ git commit -m 'Initial check-in of the profile and role
    modules'
    $ git push origin master
    ```

    You should see that the modules have been committed and pushed into a new master branch on the repository.

5. Now let's add these modules to our Puppet master. To do this, clone a clean copy of the repository onto a location on the server as the root user:

    ```
    # cd /srv
    # git clone http://localhost/git/openstack
    ```

You should receive a message such as `Cloning into 'openstack'...`, which will indicate the success of the command.

6. We'll be updating this repository with a Jenkins job, so change the ownership of the directory to the Jenkins user:

```
# chown -R jenkins:jenkins /srv/openstack
```

If you're using a remote Jenkins server, you'll need to set permissions so that you can log into this machine remotely and run a `git pull` command in that directory.

7. Next, symlink the two new puppet modules into `/etc/puppet/modules` on the master:

```
# cd /etc/puppet/modules
# ln -s /srv/openstack/puppet/modules/openstack-profile profile
# ln -s /srv/openstack/puppet/modules/openstack-role role
```

You should now see the two modules in the output of `puppet module list` on the master:

```
/etc/puppet/modules
├── openstack-profile (v0.1.0)
└── openstack-role (v0.1.0)
```

Defining the first role and profile

We already have a set of host groups defined in our design document. We'll map these directly to roles in our Puppet composition layer. Each role will get it's own class and file in the role Puppet module. A role comprises of profiles, each of which represents a piece of OpenStack functionality. For example, the `mariadb` profile will install and configure the MySQL database server for our deployment, the `amqp` profile will install and configure the RabbitMQ message server, and so on. Let's start by creating a Database Node role and associated profile.

As we mentioned earlier, we'll use the Packstack configuration that we created in `Chapter 2`, *Architecting the Cloud*, as a starting point for our composition layer. Normally, when Packstack runs, it deletes the Puppet manifests that it uses to install the OpenStack software on the hosts. If you specify the `-y` option, however, it will exit without doing anything and leave the Puppet manifests in place. On the original host that you ran Packstack in `Chapter 2`, *Architecting the Cloud*, rerun Packstack with the same answer file and the `-y` option:

```
# packstack --answer-file=packstack.answers -y
```

After the command has completed execution, it will print the name of the directory where it wrote the Puppet manifests. It should be something like `/var/tmp/packstack/20151113-214424-gIbMJA`. Descend into that directory and copy the Hiera data and manifests to your CI server.

Packstack's Puppet manifests use Hiera, Puppet's **key/value lookup tool**, to make it easy to store configuration information such as passwords and IP addresses so that they don't need to be stored in the manifests themselves. We'll stay with this practice. Copy the `hieradata` directory to `/etc/puppet/hieradata` on the CI server. To tell Puppet to reference this data, create a file called `/etc/puppet/hiera.yaml` with the following contents:

```
---
:backends:
  - yaml
:hierarchy:
  - defaults
  - "%{clientcert}"
  - "%{environment}"
  - global

:yaml:
  :datadir: /etc/puppet/hieradata
```

Now, let's create the first profile. Create a new file named `puppet/modules/openstack-profile/manifests/mariadb.pp` in our checked-out copy of the `openstack` repository. Once again, use an unprivileged account.

Starting with the Newton release of RDO, the manifests created by the Packstack tool have adopted the roles and profiles model that we're implementing in this chapter. Two roles exist in Packstack – one for controllers and one for compute nodes. We'll be creating a new role by copying relevant profiles from the controller manifest. In `mariadb.pp`, create a class definition like the following:

```
class profile::mariadb {
  include '::packstack::mariadb'
  include '::packstack::mariadb::services'
}
```

This defines the `mariadb` profile with the same Puppet code that we used to install the database in our Packstack installation. Now create a file named `puppet/modules/openstack-role/manifests/database.pp`. Create a class named `role::database` in that file, which references the profile we created earlier:

```
class role::database {
  include profile::mariadb
}
```

Add the two files to a commit and then commit and push them to the Git server.

Running the first build

Visit Jenkins at `http://jenkins:8080/`, replacing `jenkins` with the hostname of your CI server. The Jenkins UI should come up, prompting you to create a new job.

Click on **create new jobs**:

Create a new **Freestyle project** called `openstack`, as shown here:

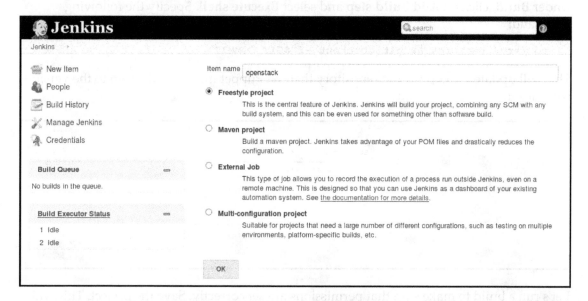

Now, we'll specify the options for the project. First, under **Source Code Management**, select
Git and specify `http://localhost/git/openstack` for your repository. (This assumes
that you're using the Git server that we set up on the CI server. If you're using a remote Git
repository, enter the clone URL for that instead.):

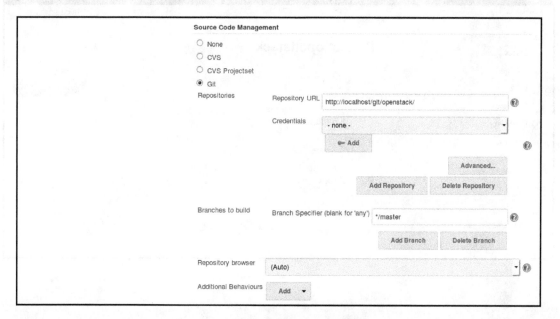

Next, we'll add a step to update the Puppet master with the latest code from the repository. Under **Build**, click on **Add build step** and select **Execute shell**. Specify the following command:

```
cd /srv/openstack && git checkout -f $GIT_COMMIT
```

This will update the copy of the repository that the Puppet master pulls from to the version we're testing:

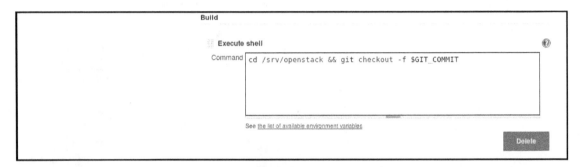

Let's run a build to make sure that permissions are set correctly. Save the project. This will bring you back to the project page. Select **Build Now**. You'll see your first build in the **Build History** tab on the bottom left:

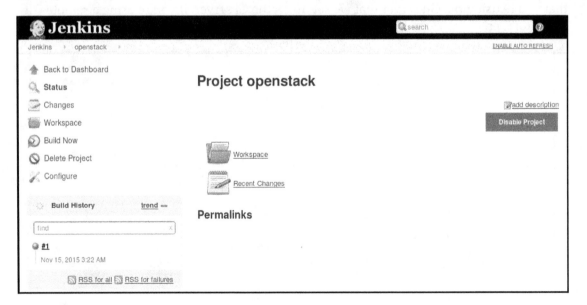

Clicking on the build number will present you with information as to whether or not the build succeeded or failed and allow you to view the console output of the build.

To verify that Jenkins pulled our new changes into the modules, look for the new files in /etc/puppet/modules:

```
# ls /etc/puppet/modules/profile/manifests/
# ls /etc/puppet/modules/role/manifests/
```

You should see the mariadb profile and the database role files in these directories.

Writing the tests

For our first test, we'll use the mysql command-line client to connect to the database we've configured and verify that we can log in using the username and password that we specified earlier. Since we're not applying the new roles and profiles to any machines, this test will fail when we run it. First, install the mysql client on the CI server. We'll use the following command to verify the connection to the database:

```
# yum install -y mariadb
```

Verify that the command was installed with the which command:

```
# which mysql
```

You should see /bin/mysql in the output.

While we could write the test directly in the configuration for the build in Jenkins, it's a best practice to include tests with the source code. Create a directory called test at the top level of the Git repository to hold the test. Use the same checked-out version of the repository that we were using before with the same unprivileged user account:

```
$ cd ~/openstack/
$ mkdir test
```

Change into the test directory and create a shell script called test.sh, which attempts to connect to MySQL on the database node. The following script will suffice for now:

```
#!/bin/sh

/bin/mysql -h db.example.com -uroot -psecret  -e "show databases;"
```

Substitute the appropriate values for the -h and -p options for your hostname and password, respectively. Running the script should result in failure:

```
$ sh test.sh
```

It should return `Can't connect to MySQL server`.

Add the `test` directory to your commit and then commit and push your changes:

```
$ cd ../
$ git add test
$ git commit -m "adding first test case"
$ git push
```

Once the code has been pushed, configure Jenkins to run the test. In the Jenkins UI, select the **openstack** project and click on **Configure** in the left-hand navigation. Under **Build**, click on **Add a build step** and select **Execute shell**. Enter the shell command, as shown in the following screenshot:

Save the configuration, and select **Build Now** from the left-hand navigation. This build should fail:

Selecting **Console Output** should show the same error that we received when we ran the command on the command line. Now let's set about configuring the database server to apply our profile and class so that the test will pass.

Assigning the first role to a system

To pull it all together, we'll start with a unconfigured system, install and configure the Puppet agent, and have it pull down the configuration that we've defined. Let's start by assigning the role to the system on the Puppet master.

As the root user on the CI server, create a `site.pp` file in `/etc/puppet/manifests`, which maps the unconfigured host to the role. For example, if my database host is named `db.example.com`, the following stanza will work:

```
node "db.example.com" {
  include role::database
}
```

On the host itself, install the RDO repository and the puppet agent with the following commands:

```
# yum install -y https://rdoproject.org/repos/rdo-release.rpm
# yum install -y puppet
```

Configure the system to use our CI server as its Puppet master. For example, if our CI server is `jenkins.example.com`, enter:

```
# puppet config set server 'jenkins.example.com' --section agent
```

Finally, do an initial Puppet run to set up the certificates:

```
# puppet agent -t
```

This should show the error `no certificate found and waitforcert is disabled`.

Log into the CI server as root and approve the certificate with the following command:

```
# puppet cert sign db.example.com
```

You will receive a notice that the certificate has been signed and the request has been removed.

Back on the database server, perform another Puppet run to pull the configuration:

```
# puppet agent -t
```

This will generate a lot of output as the system downloads all of the Puppet modules from the master. You should see the system download, install, and configure the MySQL databases for OpenStack. Finally, run a build from Jenkins again to see it succeed.

Installing Keystone

Let's iterate on the current environment, adding another profile and role. Now that we have a database available, install the first OpenStack service, Keystone. First write a unit test. Our test will ensure that we can get a token from Keystone using the admin username and password that we specified in the Packstack answer file. This can be done with a `curl` command. Create a file named `test_keystone.sh` under the `test` directory in our Git repository:

```
$ cd ~/openstack/test/
$ vi test_keystone.sh
```

Use the following content as an example, substituting your password for the password of the demo user (`secret`) and the hostname of your first controller for `controller01`:

```
curl -i \
  -H "Content-Type: application/json" \
  -d '
  { "auth": {
    "tenantId": "demo",
    "passwordCredentials": {
      "userId": "demo",
      "password": "secret"
    }
  }
}' \
http://controller01:5000/v2/auth/tokens ; echo
```

Now run the script. It should fail with a `Connection refused` error.

To make the test pass, follow a process similar to the one we used to create the database profile. Create a file named `puppet/modules/openstack-profile/manifests/keystone.pp` in the `openstack` repository with the following contents:

```
class profile::keystone {
  include '::packstack::apache'
  include '::packstack::keystone'
}
```

As before, create a role named `controller` and assign the `keystone` profile to the role.
Create a file named `puppet/modules/openstack-role/manifests/controller.pp`
with the following contents:

```
class role:controller {
  include profile::keystone
}
```

Commit and push these files into the repository:

```
$ git add puppet/modules/openstack-profile/manifests/keystone.pp
$ git add puppet/modules/openstack-role/manifests/controller.pp
$ git commit -m 'adding a controller role and keystone profile'
$ git push
```

Run the build from Jenkins again to push the files to the Puppet master. We haven't
configured Jenkins to run the new test yet, so the build should succeed, even though the test
would fail.

Once again, take an unassigned machine and assign it the role of controller based on the
hostname. In this example, we'll assign the role to a machine named
`controller01.example.com`. Edit `/etc/puppet/manifests/site.pp` on the CI server
and add the following stanza:

```
node "controller01.example.com" {
  include role::controller
}
```

On the unconfigured host named `controller01.example.com`, install the Puppet agent
and set the Puppet master:

```
# yum install -y https://rdoproject.org/repos/rdo-release.rpm
# yum install -y puppet
# puppet config set server 'jenkins.example.com' --section agent
# puppet agent -t
```

Once again, you'll need to approve the certificate on the Puppet master:

```
# puppet cert sign controller01.example.com
```

On the second Puppet run, Keystone will be installed and configured. Enable the Keystone test that we wrote as a part of the commit in Jenkins by adding a new build step such as the following:

Run the build and ensure that the test passes now that Keystone is up-and -running on the first controller.

Fully automating the pipeline

Until now, we've been manually running both the Jenkins builds and the Puppet runs. This has allowed us to ensure that we're running the tests after the Puppet runs have finished. There are a few different ways to remove these two manual steps in the pipeline.

For the Jenkins build, Jenkins can either be configured to poll the source code repository every so often, or Git can be configured to reach out to Jenkins and trigger a build when new code is pushed. Jenkins can be configured to build either when the code is pushed to any branch or only when the code is pushed to a particular branch. This can allow you to ignore work in feature branches and only perform runs on merges to a master, or it can allow you to ignore merges and only perform runs on feature branches. Tools such as Stash and Bamboo provide for even easier integration.

Managing Puppet runs is a little more complex. By default, Puppet will run every 30 minutes or so, pick up changes from the Puppet master, and apply them. While this makes sense for large environments which want to spread out the runs for performance, it can be frustrating to wait a half an hour for your environment to pick up the changes you just pushed to Git. There are two possible solutions to this problem. First, you can run Puppet on the hosts as a part of the test process. Tools such as Ansible can make this relatively simple. Second, you can decrease the interval between runs for your development environments. This is controlled by the `runinterval` setting in the `main` section of `/etc/puppet/puppet.conf`.

Once you've fully automated the pipeline, you'll want to add some kind of delay between the time that you push the changes to the Puppet master and the time that you run the unit tests. This will allow hosts to pick up the changes and implement them. For example, if you set the `runinterval` setting to 5 minutes and you expect changes to be applied within 5 minutes, you might add a build step in the Jenkins job which sleeps for 10 minutes before executing unit tests.

Summary

In this chapter, we talked about how organizations are using modern software development techniques to improve the quality of their OpenStack deployments. We built a simple deployment pipeline using Puppet, Git, and Jenkins and we used it to deploy and test two components of the OpenStack infrastructure. From here, additional components can be installed, configured, and tested in a controlled fashion.

This can seem like a lot of extra effort for folks who are used to running Packstack and getting an environment up quickly. In our experience, though, without the proper infrastructure for managing and testing changes, these deployment become unwieldy at scale. As a reminder, the three basic tenets that we're following are:

- Small, manageable changes, not large upgrade cycles
- Test-driven development
- Continuous deployments

Because most organizations will already have some experience and tooling around these principles in software development, deployment pipelines vary greatly from organization to organization. A great example infrastructure to look at is the one that the OpenStack Foundation itself uses to test changes. More information on that pipeline is available at `http ://docs.openstack.org/infra/`.

References

- OpenStack Puppet Guide: `http://docs.openstack.org/developer/puppet-openstack-guide/`
- OpenStack Ansible Project: `https://wiki.openstack.org/wiki/OpenStackAnsible`
- OpenStack Chef Project: `https://wiki.openstack.org/wiki/Chef`
- Designing Puppet – Roles and Profiles, Craig Dunn: `http://www.craigdunn.org/2012/05/239/`
- OpenStack Developer and Community Infrastructure Documentation: `http://docs.openstack.org/infra/`

5
Building to Operate

A lot of OpenStack administrators are familiar with more established virtualization platforms. They're familiar with preinstalled operations tools that will allow an administrator to simply point, click, and configure a fully robust infrastructure monitoring the solution in minutes. Unfortunately, OpenStack is not quite that simple. This doesn't mean it's inferior; quite the contrary, it's very flexible, and allows administrators to choose their own tools and configure them in a way that best suits the needs of the company or organization.

In this chapter, we will discuss day–2 operations, or in other words, what happens after the OpenStack cloud has been built, tested, and is operationally ready. It is at this point that the cloud is ready for onboard users and workloads.

Expected outcomes of this chapter

This chapter sets out to achieve the following:

- A critical insight into what is really important to monitor in an OpenStack cloud.
- A set of best practices to implement in a monitoring system. We will provide some example specifications to get you started and allow you to adjust them to meet your enterprise operation needs.
- Recommendations based on real-life examples of how to do effective capacity planning in an elastic cloud environment such as OpenStack.
- A broad understanding of some of the tools used in OpenStack operations, both open source and commercial.

Logging, monitoring, and alerting

One of the most important aspects of operating an OpenStack cloud is logging, monitoring and alerting (LMA). Since OpenStack isn't your legacy bare metal based infrastructure platform it requires a different approach. The traditional LMA methods tend to fall short when considering the scale and elasticity of an OpenStack environment. Additionally, the old binary methods of alerting "this service is down", "the resource is at 95%", or even "file system full" messages do not deliver the depth of operational information really required to know the health of an OpenStack cloud.

While there are many different tools to actually monitor log events and create alerts from the systems that run the OpenStack infrastructure, in this chapter, we will focus more on the architectural principles that will help you choose logging, monitoring, and alerting tools.

No matter what is used to do the logging, monitoring, and alerting, from an architectural standpoint, the solution should cover the following requirements:

- Provide real-time, or near real-time introspection and alerting into the OpenStack infrastructure
- Support some sort of discovery and configuration management
- Be scalable to support enterprise clouds
- Have the ability to self-monitor and the ability to be configured as highly available

Logging

An essential source of operational data for an OpenStack cloud is logs. Not only are the logs of host operating systems available, but each project running as a part of OpenStack has a separate log. However, even though they are separate, it's recommended that all logs be sent to syslog under the same syslog log level as a starting point and modified if needed.

The following is an example of a successful operation in an OpenStack log entry from `nova-api.log`:

```
2016-07-08 07:36:45.613 3474 INFO nova.osapi_compute.wsgi.server [req-
b5ff3321-19cc-4ce8-af9c-0ed59ae21ac7 f32900acc09d4898b091b2caa4900112
6f0117ddd81b4dc78a8f4ce4dd5b04f5 - - -] 10.0.3.15 "GET
/v2/6f0117ddd81b4dc78a8f4ce4dd5b04f5/flavors/1 HTTP/1.1" status: 200 len:
613 time: 0.1168451
```

For security and analysis, logs should be sent to a remote centralized syslog server. Ideally, this server will be where the log introspection, analytics, and cataloging will be done, and it should be hosted on a server with appropriate CPU and memory to support these workloads. Log introspection would be done on the content of the log entries as these logs can contain some, or all of the following (example based on the preceding log):

- Severity levels (`INFO`)
- The server that sent the log (`10.0.3.15`)
- The service that sent the log (`nova.osapi_compute.wsgi.server`)
- Metadata such as `tenant_id` and `request_id`
  (`6f0117ddd81b4dc78a8f4ce4dd5b04f5` and `req-b5ff3321-19cc-4ce8-af9c-0ed59ae21ac7`)
- Error codes from the service, and even performance data such as HTTP response times (involving limited usability for asynchronous connections due to the segmented nature of create requests and API interactions)

Here is what an error would look like:

```
nova-scheduler.log:2016-07-08 07:26:48.687 1159 ERROR
oslo.messaging._drivers.impl_rabbit [req-
c419cec6-9847-4692-8c61-733524097546 - - -
--] AMQP server on 10.0.3.15:5672 is unreachable: [Errno 111] ECONNREFUSED.
Trying
again in 4 seconds
```

As we can see above, this is a structured log file that can be parsed by many different tools to extract the severity, service, timestamp, and other relevant metadata. Furthermore, this data could be searched with open source analysis tools such as **ELK (ElasticSearch, Logstash,** and **Kibana)**. Basic information about this industry standard data mining platform can be found at `https://www.elastic.co/webinars/introduction-elk-stack`. This page also includes a webinar to get you started.

This concept of using a log processing platform, search platform, graphic dashboard, and an alerting platform is also being used as the OpenStack infrastructure monitoring solution at many large commercial and research production clouds. For example, CERN and GoDaddy are both using ELK to provide visibility into their OpenStack clouds. CERN's dashboard (`http://openstack-in-production.blogspot.com/2013/10/log-handling-and-dashboards-in-cern.html`) looks similar to this (it shows Nova API statistics):

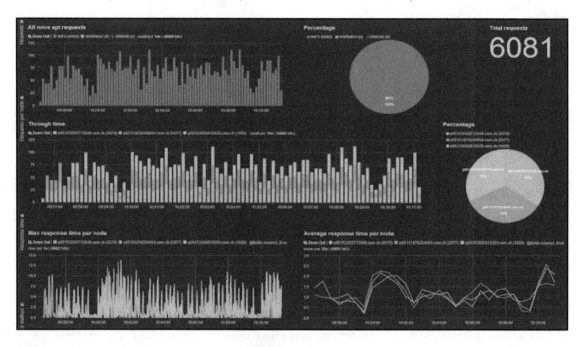

Cern OpenStack Cloud Team, 2013

However, not all solutions are ELK-based; Mirantis, for example, is distributing a product they call StackLight, which uses different log processing and formatting tools. It adds Grafana to the visual dashboard suite in addition to Kibana. Mirantis' solution also uses different components for log collection and adds InfuxDB as the database for time series data. StackLight incorporates Nagios Core into the monitoring platform to provide alerting. This stack of freeware applications is automatically configured as this monitoring platform and installed by a series of plugins (`https://www.mirantis.com/validated-solution-integrations/fuel-plugins`) to Fuel, Mirantis recently open sourced installer:

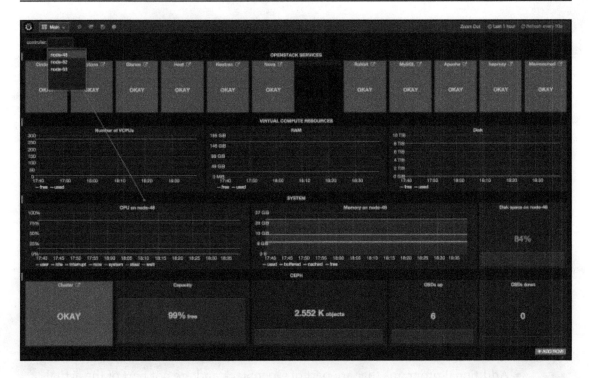

Example of Mirantis' main StackLight dashboard

Similarly, there are other distributions that have their own opinionated monitoring platforms; however, despite their differences in choices of software, they all have similar architectures and provide similar functionality to our previous examples. They are, all based on the log analysis fundamentals discussed earlier in this chapter and provide useful tools that can visualize data.

Monitoring

Many organizations struggle in the period between deployment and on-boarding of applications. Most of this struggle is due to a lack of understanding of how OpenStack cloud operations differ from a typical legacy platform. Many times, this is the hardest barrier to overcome since it requires some fundamental cultural shifts in the way engineering, operations, and developers interact with infrastructure, applications, and platforms.

While some of the practices we will cover in this section may transpose over to workload monitoring, this chapter is about operational monitoring of OpenStack infrastructure, not workloads running on OpenStack. Unlike OpenStack infrastructure, workloads running on the OpenStack cloud can be monitored by legacy platforms in many cases. There are many tools, both open source and commercial, that are purpose-built to monitor workloads running on OpenStack clouds but due to the broad availability of solutions in this sector we will not be covering that topic in this chapter. We will instead concentrate on infrastructure monitoring.

What to monitor

In general, there are many categories of processes that support management by OpenStack. They are as follows:

- Stateless services and OpenStack API endpoints such as `nova-api`, `glance-api`, and `keystone-api`, that receive user inputs.
- OpenStack service workers connected to the message bus such as `nova-scheduler`, that receives and processes user requests from other processes such as those listed earlier.

- Additional programs that are part of OpenStack and are not part of the actual codebase, but are more like enablers to the actual API layer, which provides services such as databases, replication, virtualization, and more. Some of these components are MySQL, RabbitMQ, Memcached, HAProxy, Corosync, and Pacemaker. Some of these elements are not in our Packstack environment since it is not a highly available environment; however, most production deployments by other distributions (Mirantis, Canonical, Red Hat, IBM, HP, and so on) have these or other similar tools to provide similar functions. We will briefly mention these tools as they relate to operations and monitoring later in the chapter.
- The host operating system. In your installation, you may have installed RHEL or CentOS. Both of these options need to be monitored for the standard operating system, hardware, and capacity monitoring in order to ensure the base of our install, the node itself, is operating properly. This monitoring can be an agent, IPMI, SSH, or other interfaces depending on the monitoring platform.

- Network hardware, routers, switches, firewalls, and so on will all need to be monitored; however, these are typically external to the OpenStack infrastructure and are not part of our Packstack install.
- External storage should be monitored by the respective business unit that is providing the storage to the cloud. While there are a number of options to connect storage to OpenStack nodes via fiber channel, iSCSI or NAS, monitoring this storage is beyond the scope of this book. One exception to this recommendation is made by distributed storage platforms, such as Ceph, that are often bundled with OpenStack distributions. Ceph should be monitored with the command line or tools like Calamari(Red Hat Storage Console/Tendri), Intel VSM, InkScope, ceph-dash, or OpenAttic.

Monitoring practices

The following are some distinct monitoring practices that are aimed at addressing different parts of a holistic monitoring approach an operations staff would have to handle. These practices can be classified into availability, performance, and usage. Together, these practices make up a solid foundation for any monitoring strategy. While there may be, additional components depending on industry and corporate requirements, the majority of operational use cases should fit the following ones.

Monitoring availability

Availability monitoring, at its core, is really any monitoring activity that supports the inspection of resources for OpenStack compute, storage, and networking as well as the endpoints that support the user interaction with those resources (OpenStack service APIs). Availability can be defined as simply available versus not available or as granular as specific **Service-Level Agreements (SLAs)**.

In order to measure availability, there are key metrics that can be used as indicators. They provide a status in regard to the availability of a resource, and they can also provide empirical data on how many resources are currently available. This availability check can be accomplished by running synthetic or real tests against the environment that mimic the behavior of real users.

Monitoring performance

Monitoring performance typically measures the responsiveness of a process, connection, or workflow. In cloud computing, it is typically used to define how long it takes to complete certain workflows. Some of these workflows are: creating instances, volumes, networks, or other OpenStack resources. The key metrics from the performance can usually be extracted from OpenStack service logs and the timestamps that they contain. Since provisioning an instance is a multiproject workflow, performance impacts can be traced end-to-end using start and finish times per project per request as well as between project handoffs. Other methods of measuring performance may use the output from OpenStack commands using native time measurement tools as well as by modifying the OpenStack code to add instrumentation.

Monitoring resource usage

In this section, we will only partially use resource usage monitoring. In a later section, we will cover it in more depth as it relates to capacity planning. However, the purpose of resource usage monitoring is that an operator can, at will, retrieve the amount of resources being used by not only one user, but also tenant, or the entire cloud via the OpenStack APIs. This monitoring does not have to be performed in real time. In most instances, resource monitoring is an activity done with data that has been collected over a specific period of time. Later in this chapter, we will cover the Ceilometer project, which is the metering project for OpenStack.

Alerting

The alerting process is one of the most important steps in any operational model. Alerting is the process by which the monitoring platform alerts the operator about a situation that is outside the set thresholds. These alerts can be delivered in a multitude of ways from ticketing platforms such as Remedy, e-mail, SMS, IRC, or even integrations with communication platforms such as Slack (www.slack.com). These alerts should contain the basic information regarding the event that triggered them. This could be any key value that has either gone from a good state to a non-good state or a key value that has breached an SLA level. In all cases, these alerts are driven by a change in state and may not be a direct indication of a problem, but may be an indication of a future issue.

Therefore, alerts should:

- Display which OpenStack service is affected
- Contain a general description of the change in state that caused the alert
- If implemented, have a severity level defined by the operational staff
- Have the ability to be marked as a false positive or be disabled during events such as maintenance
- Have the ability to chain alerts together in a logical fashion to trigger additional actions and provide rudimentary correlation
- Provide the ability to refer to time-series statistics such as median, percentile, and standard deviation
- Provide an instant view of services that are in a good, warning, or failed state

Believe it or not, most errors seen in a correctly configured OpenStack environment are not critical and indicate a complete outage. Most errors in OpenStack environments are usually due to failed provisions or other similar non-outage warnings. Remember, even if the OpenStack control plane has a complete failure, the workloads will continue to run (in most cases). Therefore, having a monitoring solution that can determine the proper alerting level for an error is critical. This resolves issues of overalerting operations personnel and causing them to troubleshoot minor warnings when in reality these warnings may be simply an indication of something minor and should be watched as a trend indicator. A simple requirement would consist of a policy similar to the following points:

- Critical errors, resulting in failure states, should always be reported in an alert and require immediate action
- Other problems in OpenStack HA environments, for example, one failed service on one controller in an environment with three controllers, should not be marked as critical, but marked as a warning or deferred state to indicate a degradation of high availability

A great way to test the capacity of an OpenStack cloud before it is placed into production, or on a staging cloud that is built to mirror the production environment, is to run a load generator against it. One open source project, named Rally(`http://rally.readthedoc s.io/en/latest/index.html`),is a great tool to identify functional failures and performance bottlenecks in your environment. The following figure describes the basic functions of the tool:

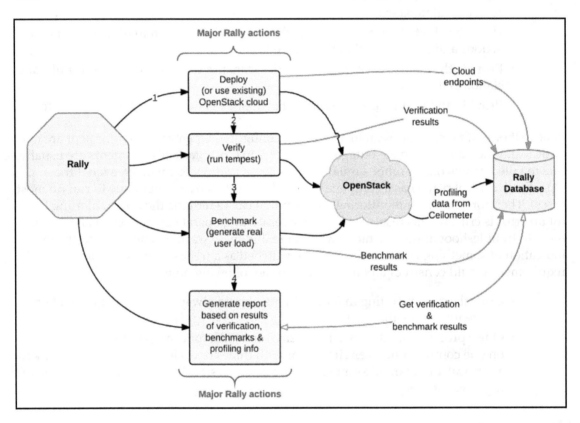

Rally Actions – Copyright 2016 OpenStack Foundation

Active monitoring

There are quite a few activities to monitor in OpenStack. In general, there are three major areas to monitor:

- OpenStack services (required for orchestration and provisioning)
- Processes (the actual running processes of OpenStack components)
- HA control cluster (the components providing HA capability to the cloud)

Services

Checking services is all about availability. If a service is down, cloud users will be faced with errors that prevent them from using the APIs and, furthermore, interacting with the cloud. These service checks should be performed regularly using simulated transactions generated from the monitoring platform. We call these simulated because they do not require all the specific customizations of the image and post deployment configuration that may be needed for real workloads. While using real workloads is possible, it is less desirable due to the additional overhead needed to run actual transactions on a regular basis in addition to the real deployment load. Synthetic transactions should be launched from a dedicated user in their own project with strict quotas. This way the transactions can be tracked using tenant and user IDs that are separate from real traffic.

These checks should be launched against the VIP addresses for endpoints (if configured in an HA configuration) and only report two possible options: completed or failed. This way, the tests can be contained to simple operations. Complex simulations will involve other endpoints and may provide false positives. For example, if the Nova API endpoint were to be tested, a good test would be to check the flavors associated with the monitoring tenant. An example call to the API to the Nova project would be as follows:

```
GET /v2.1/{tenant_id}/flavors
```

Additional API specifications can be found at http://developer.openstack.org/.

In order to make this API call via a monitoring platform such as Nagios, the platform could be configured to use the nova CLI client for the Nova project from a plugin script, or a set of plugin scripts, which would call the API via Python or another scripted language. These plugin scripts, many of which are available for free at `http://www.nagios.com`, can be leveraged to check the API endpoint status using simulated actions. For example, some OpenStack infrastructure plugins have been contributed to the Nagios directory such as the one called `check_nova_api` from *Rakesh Patnaik* at `https://github.com/rakesh-patnaik/nagios-openstack-monitoring`, which checks the API service for Nova using Python and a direct call to the Nova API endpoint. The `nagios-openstack-monitoring` plugins not only have the capabilities to monitor the API endpoints but the plugin also contains scripts to check the processes.

Processes

Many individual processes support the operation of OpenStack. Many of these processes run on the controller nodes and need to be running in order to provide API availability (the `nova-api` process) as well as processes that coordinate functionality to other parts of the control stack (mariaDB and RabbitMQ). These processes can be checked locally, through remote SSH agents driven by shell scripts, or through automation enabled by software such as Ansible, Chef, and Puppet. Additionally, as aforementioned, there are plugins for monitoring platforms, such as Nagios, ZenOs, and Zabbix, that also include these process checks.

HA control cluster

Many different distributions use HAProxy to enable active/active availability across multiple OpenStack control servers (a minimum of three). This HAProxy service acts as a reverse-proxy and simple load balancer configured to listen to VIP addresses in front of the OpenStack endpoint addresses. It is common practice to have HAProxy running on each one of the controller nodes in an HA cluster. Since the HAProxy service is tied to the VIP addresses configured for the OpenStack API services, if these services fail under HAProxy, then HAProxy itself will fail over to another controller node for the service. However, HAProxy does not monitor or fail over the processes nor does it move the VIP addresses to other cluster members. Therefore, an additional tool such as pacemaker or keepalived should be used to satisfy this requirement.

The following figure shows a logical diagram of one way to configure HA controllers:

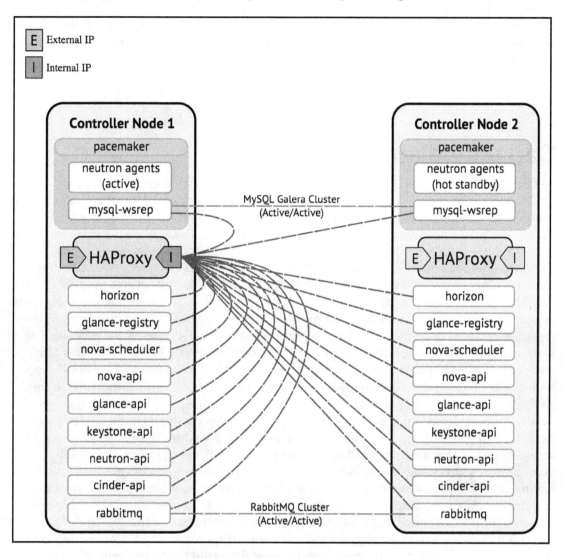

Mirantis OpenStack controller HA architecture – Mirantis

More information on this topic can be found at `http://docs.openstack.org/ha-guide/controller-ha-haproxy.html`. Alternatively, there is also the ability to use other external software or hardware load balancers instead of HAProxy.

Given this architecture for HA, and the monitoring of processes on each of the HA control nodes, it is possible that in a three-node cluster, two of the three controllers' processes for a single project can be completely down and OpenStack still be completely functional. This is why, as in service monitoring, process states and overall health alerts must be customized very carefully. Simply because one controller's individual process (for example, `nova-api`) fails and the HA infrastructure is still operational, does not mean that the monitoring solution should display a critical alert that the OpenStack cloud has failed.

Capacity planning

As one of the four major ITIL processes that fall under financial management for IT, capacity planning is clearly an important part of any cloud strategy. However, not all cloud strategies are the same. It is very important to differentiate workloads in enterprise virtualization and in an OpenStack elastic cloud. With virtualization, each workload, and in many cases each server, is important. If an individual virtualization server becomes overused or is somehow degraded, that particular server is investigated, scaled, and/or repaired. One common analogy is to compare virtualized VMs and servers to "pets". In the pure OpenStack cloud world, there is no such construct for these individual instances (pets) except when virtualized workloads are moved into the elastic cloud and thus bring IT-as-a-service workloads into a true cloud. OpenStack was constructed around the premise that workloads are ephemeral, failure is expected, and growth should be scaled horizontally, not vertically. If a workload fails, another will simply be started in its place. "Livestock" has been the analogy used to explain this idea of ephemeral instances and workloads. In this analogy, livestock are simply a resource; if they die, or are irreparably injured, they are simply destroyed and replaced. In OpenStack, this idea even extends to the underlying hardware. In many companies, compute servers are simply white label hardware compute server resources that are to be used on-demand. If they fail, other, online and equally ubiquitous resources take their place (either in a scripted disaster recovery fashion or by having adequate excess capacity). Furthermore, if the compute servers become slow due to high loads, more ubiquitous resources (compute servers) are added to increase capacity. This is an important concept to grasp when speaking about elastic capacity. Under this definition of compute servers as generically uniform, disposable, and scalable resources, when the available capacity changes, growth is not linear but based on demand. However, demand can change with development cycles, development methodologies, time of the year, and production cycles.

This variability of demand is typically linear and possibly exponential based on cloud adoption. However, proper methodologies are required when constructing an OpenStack environment to help develop the most accurate capacity planning and provide a foundation to create strategic and tactical decisions later. This differs quite a bit from virtualization capacity planning, which tends to be more linear since the workloads are more persistent and are not recycled very frequently.

Planning your city

Very similar to civil planning and architecture, the OpenStack cloud is a city of tenants that require resources to exist. However, with limited resources, tenants cannot be left to self-manage; the risk of resource exhaustion is too great. This would be analogous to the residents of an apartment building having unlimited power, water, gas, cable, and space without metering or charging for anything. Many residents would probably operate under the assumption that the resources were unlimited and they could oversize and oversubscribe to everything without consequence. Therefore, it is up to operations, both in civil engineering and OpenStack clouds, to do capacity management and risk mitigation for the end user. This means finding a way to track, analyze, and gather payment (or at least show costs) from end users or their tenant cost center. This includes creating packages of structured resources that are predetermined, which users can select from as well as creating and maintaining a quota system.

Capacity risk mitigation and planning are done by performing three distinct actions:

- Track usage
- Analyze growth
- Chargeback/showback

Tracking usage and analyzing growth

In order to track usage of any resource, we first need to standardize the units we plan to count. In cloud computing, extreme granularity is possible using the data that exists in OpenStack databases, as well as using the metering project Ceilometer. While there are many different meters that can be tracked, let's start by tracking the number of individual vCPUs used over time, amounts of memory over time, and disk usage down to the minute. However, letting users put together their own combinations of these three data points can result in tens of thousands of combinations. Therefore, in the OpenStack cloud, we use flavors to limit user choices. Flavors are virtual hardware templates that are logical groupings of compute, storage, and even network elements.

This simplifies the chargeback/showback equation by logically grouping resources into manageable offerings. In our examples, we will only be considering vCPU and memory; however, the same principles can be applied to persistent and ephemeral storage as well as network resource allocation.

Continuing with our analogy of civil engineering, we can think of a flavor as an extended family looking to occupy an apartment building with a set of space requirements. In this example, one constraint we will have is that the 65,536 sq/ft building can only have a maximum of 16 rooms and by code, can only hold 64 people. However, since this is a new apartment building, the room sizes have not been determined and the property manager will build the rooms to match the family's requirements. The property manager decides to let the first three applicants pick sizes for their rooms and he will bill them for whatever specifications the families need.

Let's start with each family's requests, each with exact and unique requirements:

- 3-person family requiring 1,024 square feet
- 7-person family requiring 8,096 square feet
- 29-person family requiring 30,720 square feet

Below we can see what a sample 65,536 sq/ft house would look like using these unique and arbitrary room sizes:

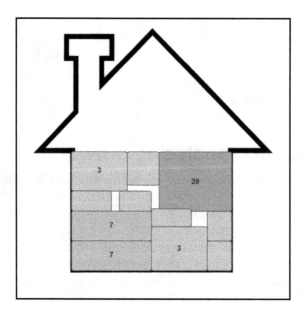

We now have a total of 49 people and their belongings occupying the building with a capacity of 64. That leaves room for 15 more people spread across a lot of wasted space (resources) of all types and configurations since no more of the existing family groupings listed above fit nicely into equal rooms in the existing space; the property manager only has two choices. He can create additional odd-sized apartments to fit 15 more people of different families and hope that families of that size apply, or buy a new house and continue to use the existing odd sizes while abandoning the wasted space in the property. This is what happens in an OpenStack cloud when flavor standardization does not take place.

Consider a compute node as a cargo van and flavors as boxes. With standard size boxes come ease of packing and high efficiency. Consider the boxes as vCPUs; for now, we will consider the boxes all square with the following measurements:

- 1-ft wide box
- 2-ft wide box
- 4-ft wide box

Most of the boxes people ship on this route are of the 2-ft flavor, but two other types of boxes are also available (1 foot and 4 foot). However, the Department of Transportation only allows 64 feet of boxes per truck. However, this time we created spaces that were stackable. We can now see what happens when we have structured groupings of boxes that are exponents of one another:

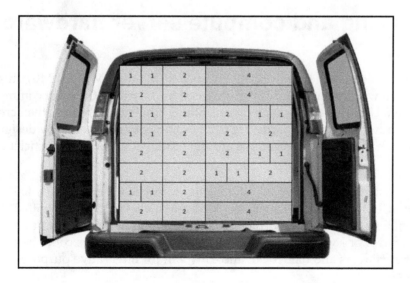

As you can see, we now have 64ft of boxes in the cargo van; since we've controlled our box (flavor) sizings and made them standard, we make it easy for the cargo loader (or in OpenStack's case, resource management programs such as `nova-scheduler/cinder-scheduler`) to do the placement. We are no longer wasting a lot of resources or space. As a result, efficiency is increased. Since efficiency is high, capacity planning becomes much easier and more predictable.

Of course, the preceding example used only one resource for sizing, vCPU. The sizing becomes more difficult when we add RAM and, possibly storage sizing, with each OpenStack flavor. We can think of flavors as nesting tables. In order to get the most efficiency, the tables have to be a fraction of the largest size. Another way to think of this is packing a box with the smaller boxes. If you can fit many combinations of the smaller boxes in the larger box, with no wasted space, you have a winning flavor combination. OpenStack flavor resources should follow these same recommendations:

- Determine the most common flavor in use in your organization today
- Double (t x 2) the most used flavor and it will be your largest offering (double any resources that need to fit the nesting method for capacity planning)
- Halve (tx 0.5) the most used flavor and it will be your smallest offering
- If you have additional flavors that are larger or smaller, increase or decrease by this same amount

Flavor sizing and compute server hardware selection

Since typical workloads call for multiples of 2 in vCPU and RAM (1024 MB), this works out particularly well when the compute hardware is sized based on the most common flavor of an organization. Unfortunately, many organizations buy hardware first, then create OpenStack clouds; others reuse hardware from existing environments. By designing compute server hardware configurations around workloads, maximum efficiency can be gained.

For example, an average flavor in an organization could be a 2 vCPU with 4096 MB of RAM. Doubling of this common flavor would result in a 4 vCPU flavor with 8192 MB of RAM. The smallest flavor would then be calculated at half of the middle flavor (one-fourth of the largest flavor at 1 vCPU and 2048 MB of RAM). Other flavors could be added above and below these flavors and named XL and Tiny, but for illustrative purposes, we will stick with only three.

In order to determine compute capacity, we use the desired VM density that is desired; for this discussion we will set the estimate at 40 VMs per compute server and multiply the density by the organization's most common flavor:

40 x 2 vCPU = 80 vCPU (assuming non-hyperthreaded CPU, multiply this number by 1.3 for hyperthreading)

40 x 4096 = 160 GB RAM (assuming a 1:1 ratio of RAM subscription)

As a rule of thumb, compute nodes require about 20% of the total vCPU and RAM for overhead and OS processes when fully loaded. These resources need to be included in the calculations for total resources needed:

Required number of vCPUs with OS overhead: 80 * 1.20 (100% + 20%) = 96 vCPU

Required memory with OS overhead: 160 * 1.20 = 192 GB RAM

Therefore, in order to have an accurately scaled starting point, we would need a compute server with the hardware to support 96 vCPUs. We will set the overcommit ratio at 8:1 for vCPUs, therefore we would need to divide the number of required vCPUs by 8 to get the number of the CPU cores we need. Overcommit ratios may vary, so adjust your calculation to match, as shown here:

Total number of vCPUs needed / Overcommit = Cores

96 / 8 = 12 CPU cores

Therefore, based on this calculation, we need 12 CPU cores for about 40 instances of the average flavor of this cloud, named medium. Since most servers come as dual–core or quad-core models now, we would simply need a single dual core CPU with a 6-core processor. For this example, something like the Intel E5-2620v3 or E5-2643v3 would be sufficient for generalized workloads.

For memory, we simply need to ensure that each compute server has 192 GB of RAM, and since this is a 6-dual-core single CPU server with 12 DIMM banks, each bank would require 32 GB per processor bank. Therefore, as a visual representation, the following figure is roughly what the logical memory allocation could look like.

There are some spare resources remaining after the server has reached its 40-instance limit plus one. This memory could be used for an additional instance or left as a reserve for compute server OS spikes at a load.

COMPUTE SERVER - 192GB RAM - 2 X 2643 INTEL CPU (96 vCPUs @ 8:1 OverSub)

S S	L	M	M	L	
S S		M	M		
M	S S	M	S S	S S	
M	S S	M	S	M	
L	M	L	M	M	
	M		M	M	
M	M	M	M	
M	M	M	M	

OS Reserved CPU

In the preceding figure, we have a breakdown as shown here:

Flavor size	Instances	vCPUs	Memory (GB)
Small	13	13	26
Medium	24	48	96
Large	4	16	32
Total	41	78	154
Reserved for OS		18(~20%)	38 GB(~20%)

This shows an almost ideal configuration for our earlier flavor requirements, even though we didn't fill it with *all* medium-sized images. However, if more flavors had been added without adhering to the recommended preceding model, we would end up with gaps and wasted CPU and memory depending on the flavor diversity and number of instances of those flavors.

Using this flavor determinism as a best practice will allow operators to more accurately measure/monitor the following:

- Overall capacity
- Growth over time
- Utilization and overutilization
- Correct VM placement by Nova

Many companies have spent considerable time developing in-house strategies for collecting, managing, and analyzing data from their clouds to answer the topics discussed. However, in recent years, many different **Cloud Management Platforms(CMPs)** and purpose-built monetization and management software have emerged to simplify chargeback and showback. However, there have been scale challenges around OpenStack's telemetry project Ceilometer. Advances in technology have been made; however, some capacity planning software is now configured to use the OpenStack APIs directly and does not even need the OpenStack telemetry service (Ceilometer).

Capacity in the cloud must be part of a more deterministic type of capacity planning methodology. Keeping the appropriate elasticity at all times is a tricky business and must be carefully monitored to achieve a balance between availability and depreciation of resources. Users tend to believe that cloud resources are infinite; sadly, however they are not. All requests for resources, even paravirtualized ones, are simply mapped back to groups of physical devices that have limits. Unfortunately, end users tend to not know or somehow forget this paradigm. As a result, at times, end users fall back into a hoarding behavior when they are not charged or tracked for resource consumption. Unfortunately, this behavior is most likely the byproduct of years of legacy infrastructure processes taking months before developer teams were able to obtain additional infrastructure. With these limits and demands in mind, it is increasingly important for cloud administration or operations to take charge of capacity planning for all aspects of the OpenStack cloud. The easiest way to take charge of this behavior is through chargeback or showback. This allows OpenStack administrators to give users an account of what they are consuming on a regular basis. Additionally, if chargeback is enabled, it is a way for cloud groups or public providers to recoup the costs of maintaining an elastic environment.

In order to be able to show and charge users for resources, administrators need to follow the preceding capacity planning recommendations as well as providing cloud users with features such as periodic statements, the cost for resources before deploying, running costs, and payment or billing options. While most software that can perform this functionality is in the commercial realm, there are a few open source tools that can be leveraged to provide some features.

Some examples of leading capacity planning and chargeback solutions are as follows:

Name	Company	Open/closed source	Supports	Website
CloudKitty	Objectif Libre	Open source	OpenStack	`https://wiki.openstack.org/wiki/CloudKitty`
HP	Cloud Optimizer 3.0	Closed source	OpenStack AWS Xen VMware Hyper-V	`http://www8.hp.com/us/en/software-solutions/capacity-planning-server-virtualization-management/`
Red Hat	Cloudforms ManageIQ	Closed source Open source	OpenStack AWS Google	`https://access.redhat.com/documentation/en/red-hat-cloudforms/4.1/http://manageiq.org/`

Talligent	OpenBook 3.0	Closed source	OpenStack AWS VMware	`http://talligent.com /openbook-faqs/`

Backups and recovery

Typically, backups and recovery aren't the first things traditional OpenStack operators think of. This is usually because of the ephemeral workloads traditionally run on OpenStack clouds, which really didn't persist long enough to be backed up. However, as OpenStack adoption has grown exponentially, we are seeing more and more production OpenStack deployments that include persistent workloads, especially in IT-as-a-service clouds. As a result, a need has arisen to back up critical infrastructure data as well as persistent workloads running on the cloud.

Infrastructure backup architecture

While workloads running on an OpenStack cloud are the stars of the show, the infrastructure is the real hero. Keeping the APIs available and running 100% without interruption should be the end goal of any operator when it comes to availability. However, it's simply not reality. Even with proper life-cycle management and change procedures, data corruption can happen. Since the heart of OpenStack is a structured database running on mariaDB, it only makes sense to run it in a highly available configuration. However, what happens if, during operation, errors are made and are replicated across all HA nodes? Failure. Now, without backup and recovery, not only are the APIs offline, workloads could still be online, but all the data about every instance and the network configuration for those instances are lost. This is a true disaster for any OpenStack cloud.

Backup strategies – what to backup

There is some critical data that must be backed up regularly in order to ensure proper recovery of OpenStack cloud. The frequency of these backups should align with your recovery time objective (the time to cloud restoration after a disaster in order to avoid unacceptable consequences to business continuity). There may also be recovery point objectives and SLAs within your organization that you may have to adhere to. While these are more common to disaster recovery regarding persistent workloads and not the infrastructure, there are always exceptions.

Critical items you should back up to be able to recover from a full or partial disaster are listed in the following table:

Data item	Project	Location	Instructions
MySQL DB	Openstack DB	Controller	Use `mysqldump` to export the contents of the database. Copy the data to a backup server.
Nova	Compute	Compute controller	Make copies of `/etc/nova` and copy to the backup server. Make copies of `/var/lib/nova` except `/var/lib/nova/instances` on compute nodes. Instance backups will be discussed later.
Glance	Image Repo	Controller	Copy the `/etc/glance` and `/var/lib/glance` directories. Or rsync `/var/lib/glance/images` to another backup server.
Keystone	Identity	Controller	Back up `/etc/keystone`. Back up `/var/lib/keystone` if there is any data in it.
Cinder	Block Storage	Controller	Back up `/etc/cinder`. Back up `/var/lib/cinder`.
Swift	Object Storage	Controller	Back up `/etc/swift`; it contains the configuration files as well as the ring and ring builder files. Without these, your data is completely inaccessible. Copy these to every storage node before backing them up.

Once all of these files have been backed up and moved to a secure on-site or off-site disaster recovery server, in order to restore your OpenStack cloud you will basically need to stop all services on the existing cloud, copy all of the files back into place, recover the database from the export, and restart the cloud.

While this looks simple, it takes time. If this plan looks like it won't meet your RTO needs, there are ways to make OpenStack highly available and create an architecture that is both multicloud and multiregion while having the ability to fail over and recover to a completely different site during a disaster. These solutions involve replication of Cinder storage across WAN links, a custom migration middleware solution, and a network plan to bring up the disaster recovery cloud online with all of the access and configurations it needs to satisfy business requirements. This solution can be extended by replicating database metadata and having a global object store for Glance images; however, as one can imagine, this is quite a feat of architecture and engineering and beyond the scope of this book.

Workload backup architecture

As mentioned previously, workloads are the reason that a cloud even exists. In a perfect world, all applications would be cloud-native, fully distributed, and 12 factor apps. They wouldn't require backups because they would be regionally or globally distributed across multiple clouds and horizontally scaled to autoscale in the case of a disaster in one location. However, that is simply not the reality for many organizations. Many organizations have the need to run persistent workloads and traditional applications in production clouds. However, the legacy methods of backing up these applications, especially in bare metal environments, are drastically different. With most resources being virtualized and tenant networks isolated, traditional backup and restore architectures simply do not apply in OpenStack. Therefore, not only do organizations need a disaster recovery backup solution for workloads, but they also need operational backup solutions sometimes known as **Backup-as-a-Service (BaaS)**.

Planning for disaster recovery

Since workloads that require back up on OpenStack consist mainly of persistent instances; we must backup all parts of the instance, not only the disk image(s) that hold all of the runtime and persistent data but also the metadata that is required to make that workload instance(s) able to be restored from backup. However, OpenStack lacks the ability to provide a policy-based, automated, comprehensive backup and recovery solution. While OpenStack provides a patchwork of tools and APIs to provide some sort of backup effort, even tools such as OpenStack's Cinder API, which provides support for taking full and incremental volume snapshots are still disruptive and the workload has to be taken offline to take a snapshot or risk data corruption.

To illustrate this, we can look at the typical steps to do a simple backup on a basic workload:

1. Pause instances.
2. Detach Cinder volumes (root volume and any additional nonroot volumes).
3. Take an instance snapshot for each instance and store it in Glance for later retrieval.
4. Use Cinder to backup all the aforementioned volumes and place them in Object Storage (Swift/Ceph).
5. Document these copies since OpenStack does not track them for you.
6. Resume instances.

These steps are very command-intensive, take time, require custom scripts, and since there is a manual documentation step could be error-prone. These steps may also not adhere to existing internal backup policies of the organization.

This manual type of backup operation is antiquated and feature-limited. Any enterprise-level backup solution should be non-impacting, able to do incremental backups and be customized for each workload, and able to span multiple instances when workloads are also spread across instances. Additionally, tenants should be able to easily back up their own workloads and test them before committing them to storage and have the ability to restore and replay backups when they desire. Workload backup software should also be able to provide a disaster recovery component so that in the event of a catastrophe, backed-up and replicated resources are available at different geographic locations in case any single location is compromised.

There are few open source and commercial options when considering workload backup solutions that use native snapshots from OpenStack. One open source option is called Raksha (`https://wiki.openstack.org/wiki/Raksha`), the OpenStack project version of what became TrilioVault (`http://www.triliodata.com/about/`), a commercial data protection, backup, and disaster recovery specifically designed for OpenStack. Trilio Data has taken the previously mentioned workload backup snapshot procedure and designed a flexible and scalable solution. Using TrilioVault, both full and incremental backups of snapshots can be stored on a wide range of storage including NFS, Swift, and other third-party arrays. Recovery is also GUI-driven and simplifies what would otherwise be driven by sets of homegrown scripts to launch backup and recovery actions. TrilioVault also provides additional features for data retention, protection, and data integrity.

Additionally, traditional file-based backup solutions can be run inside OpenStack and can be used as Backup-as-a-Service (BaaS) offerings. While we can't cover every Backup-as-a-Service option, the following table compares some common options from some software used by enterprise customers today. This BaaS model is typically used by cloud providers, both public and private, to offer backup services to clients. These are priced with a cost model based on capacity, bandwidth, the number of clients, and so on. Cloud backup services leverage the shared private cloud infrastructure, just like other cloud services and are infrastructure-abstracted. BaaS can be leveraged by both tenants inside the cloud as well as external hosts that desire to back up into the cloud.

Features and common requirements	Zmanda	Cloudberry	Commvault Simpana	Community Amanda (open source)
File-based backup	Yes	Yes	Yes	Yes
Client-server architecture	Yes	Can be both	Yes	Yes
Data formats available	Native dump and/or GNU tar	Swift Object Storage	Native dump/SCSI	Native dump and/or GNU tar
Deduplication	No	Yes	Yes	No
DR to remote site	Yes	Yes	Yes	No
Encryption and compression	Yes	Yes	Yes	Yes
Incremental backups	Yes	No	Yes	Yes
LDAP integration	Yes	Workaround	Yes	Workaround
Licensing	Annual or Multiyear	Annual, Permanent	Annual	Free
Linux client	Yes	No	Yes	Yes
MS Exchange	Yes	Yes	Yes	Workaround
MS SharePoint	Yes	Workaround	Yes	Workaround
MS SQL	Yes	Yes	Yes	Workaround
Operational GUI	Yes	Yes	Yes	No
Reporting	Yes	Limited capacity	Yes	No

Restore to different location	Yes	Yes	Yes	Yes
Restore to individual DBs	Yes	Yes	Yes	No
Specify retention time	Yes	Yes	Yes	Yes
Windows client	Yes	Yes	Yes	Yes

Summary

In this chapter, we discussed topics that are critical to the operation of an OpenStack cloud. We covered tactical ways to monitor, plan, and backup your cloud; this is simply the beginning. There are many great resources online that can assist you in the operation of an OpenStack cloud; however, I suggest that readers start with the actual OpenStack operations and architecture guides. These are located at `http://docs.openstack.org/ops/` and `http://docs.openstack.org/arch/`, respectively. These guides will provide all the required foundational information to help make operations in any cloud journey a success.

In the next chapter, you will be learning about integrating existing business and operational processes such as identity management integration and unit testing using Jenkins.

References

- `http://docs.openstack.org/arch/`
- `http://openstack-in-production.blogspot.com/2013/10/log-handling-and-dashboards-in-cern.html`
- `https://www.mirantis.com/validated-solution-integrations/fuel-plugins`
- `http://www.slack.com`
- `http://rally.readthedocs.io/en/latest/index.html`
- `http://developer.openstack.org/`
- `http://www.nagios.com`
- `https://github.com/rakesh-patnaik/nagios-openstack-monitoring`

- http://docs.openstack.org/ha-guide/controller-ha-haproxy.html
- https://wiki.openstack.org/wiki/CloudKitty
- http://www8.hp.com/us/en/software-solutions/capacity-planning-server-virtualization-management/
- https://access.redhat.com/documentation/en/red-hat-cloudforms/4.1/
- http://manageiq.org/
- http://talligent.com/openbook-faqs/
- https://wiki.openstack.org/wiki/Raksha
- http://www.triliodata.com/about/
- http://docs.openstack.org/ops/
- https://www.elastic.co/webinars/introduction-elk-stack

6
Integrating the Platform

One of the OpenStack architects we've worked with is fond of saying, "No OpenStack implementation is an island". Each deployment integrates with the legacy IT infrastructure around it, from identity management systems to auditing systems to billing systems. OpenStack's standardized APIs make these integrations relatively simple. This chapter will cover the integration points available within an OpenStack implementation and many of the common integration patterns.

In this chapter, we'll look at the following points in detail:

- **Identity management(IdM)** integration
- Provisioning workflows
- Metering and billing

These three different platform integrations demonstrate the three prominent integration patterns for OpenStack. Integrating Keystone with an IdM system such as Active Directory is relatively prescriptive – as Cinder is designed to integrate with storage arrays, Keystone is designed to integrate with IdM systems. The contract between Keystone and the IdM system is largely hidden in the code of the project.

The other two integration patterns demonstrate two different ways to interact externally with the OpenStack system. External provisioning workflows drive the OpenStack system through its REST API. They either interact directly with the Neutron, Cinder, Nova, and Glance APIs or they leverage the Heat orchestration API to create, modify, and delete objects within the OpenStack deployment. In contrast, metering, billing, and auditing systems interact with the output of the system by either listening in on the OpenStack message bus for events to occur or by consuming events from the Event API.

IdM integration

In a 2014 blog post, OpenStack developer *Nathan Kinder* famously (and convincingly) argued that **Keystone is not an authentication service**. In this post, Kinder describes the deployment pattern of placing the `Keystone` service behind an Apache HTTP server, which uses native modules to perform authentication. Kinder makes two arguments in his post:

- Most people use some kind of external authentication system with OpenStack
- The reference authentication system (the SQL plugin) doesn't have any of the features that we'd expect from an authentication service

Both of these arguments have been proven in our experience; the first integration that most of the organizations we work with tackle is that of the IdM service.

Authentication and authorization in OpenStack

Having an understanding of how authentication and authorization work within OpenStack is helpful. Each call to an OpenStack API service is authorized by a bearer token, which is retrieved from and verified by the `Keystone` service. The following figure summarizes this interaction:

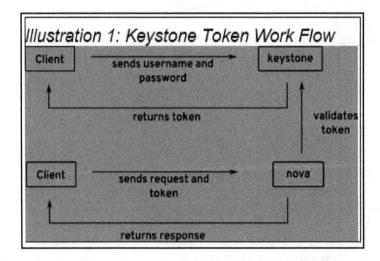

When requesting the token from Keystone, the client sends along the requested scope of the token: the tenant, project, or domain. Assuming that the credentials authorize the client, the token that Keystone returns is specific to the scope requested. Once the client has obtained the token, each API request to the other OpenStack services contains the token in an HTTP header. The other services use that token to authorize the requests from the client.

There are two versions of the Keystone API in wide use in OpenStack at present: versions 2 and 3. In version 2 of the API, users are authorized to specific projects or **tenants**. A user may have privileges in more than one tenant and the privileges may vary by tenant. For example, the user **msolberg** may have administrative privileges in the **msolberg** tenant, but only user privileges in the **architect** tenant. Version 3 of the API introduces the concept of authorization domains, which provide a hierarchy above basic tenancy. Version 3 of the Keystone API has been around for a few releases, but it has taken some time for each of the services to support the new authorization model. As such, most OpenStack deployments still use the Keystone v2 API.

Keystone uses a combination of backend drivers when deciding whether or not to issue a token when presented with a set of credentials. The first backend driver is the identity driver. The identity driver can either be SQL (the reference implementation) or **Lightweight Directory Access Protocol** (**LDAP**). If the driver is set to LDAP, an external directory service can be used to authenticate users. The second driver is the **assignment** driver. This driver allows users to authenticate using LDAP and assign roles using the SQL database. This configuration is the most commonly used integration pattern for Active Directory.

Configuring Keystone with split assignment and identity

Before configuring Keystone to use Active Directory (or other LDAP services) for authentication, a few changes will need to be made on the Active Directory side. First, decide on mapping objects in Active Directory to the accounts in OpenStack. For example, you may want any user who has an account in the directory to have access to a tenant in OpenStack, or you may want to restrict usage to a particular group of users. If you intend to restrict users, you will need to create a group or attribute to filter them. Second, a user who has the ability to do a look up on other users needs to be created. Perform a test that validates that the user has the ability to read the appropriate subtree of account objects using a utility such as `ldapsearch`. For more information on the prerequisites for the Active Directory side, refer to `https://wiki.openstack.org/wiki/HowtoIntegrateKeystonewithAD`.

Next, we will configure Keystone to use the LDAP identity backend and the SQL assignment backend. Packstack supports this configuration out-of-the-box, and we only need to update the Hiera data on our Puppet master for our installation to reflect the new settings. The following table represents the settings that will be required:

Hiera variable	keystone.conf setting	Description
`CONFIG_KEYSTONE_IDENTITY_BACKEND`	`identity.driver`	That backend to use (`ldap`)
`CONFIG_KEYSTONE_LDAP_URL`	`ldap.url`	The URI for the AD LDAP service
`CONFIG_KEYSTONE_LDAP_USER_DN`	`ldap.user`	The service user for looking up accounts
`CONFIG_KEYSTONE_LDAP_USER_PASSWORD`	`ldap.password`	The password for the service user
`CONFIG_KEYSTONE_LDAP_SUFFIX`	`ldap.suffix`	The suffix for the service account
`CONFIG_KEYSTONE_LDAP_USER_SUBTREE`	`ldap.user_tree_dn`	The tree containing user accounts in AD
`CONFIG_KEYSTONE_LDAP_USER_OBJECTCLASS`	`ldap.user_objectclass`	The object class for user accounts (`person`)
`CONFIG_KEYSTONE_LDAP_USER_FILTER`	`ldap.user_filter`	An optional filter to use or selecting only certain users in the tree
`CONFIG_KEYSTONE_LDAP_USER_ID_ATTRIBUTE`	`ldap.user_id_attribute`	The attribute to use as the Keystone user ID (`cn`)
`CONFIG_KEYSTONE_LDAP_USER_NAME_ATTRIBUTE`	`ldap.user_name_attribute`	The attribute to use as the Keystone user name (`cn`)
`CONFIG_KEYSTONE_LDAP_USER_MAIL_ATTRIBUTE`	`ldap.user_mail_attribute`	The attribute to use as the Keystone user e-mail (`mail`)
`CONFIG_KEYSTONE_LDAP_USER_ENABLED_ATTRIBUTE`	`ldap.user_enabled_attribute`	The attribute that determines whether a user is enabled or not (`userAccountControl`)
`CONFIG_KEYSTONE_LDAP_USER_ENABLED_MASK`	`ldap.user_enabled_mask`	The bitmask to use to determine whether the account is enabled (`2`)
`CONFIG_KEYSTONE_LDAP_USER_ENABLED_DEFAULT`	`ldap.user_enabled_default`	The default value to use to determine whether the account is enabled (`512`)
`CONFIG_KEYSTONE_LDAP_USER_ATTRIBUTE_IGNORE`	`ldap.user_attribute_ignore`	Attributes to ignore on the object (`password`, `tenant_id`, `tenants`)

CONFIG_KEYSTONE_LDAP_USER_ALLOW_CREATE	ldap.user_allow_create	Whether or not we can create users (False)
CONFIG_KEYSTONE_LDAP_USER_ALLOW_UPDATE	ldap.user_allow_update	Whether or not we can update users (False)
CONFIG_KEYSTONE_LDAP_USER_ALLOW_DELETE	ldap.user_allow_delete	Whether or not we can delete users (False)

Once the appropriate settings have been determined for your environment, update `/etc/puppet/heiradata/defaults.yaml` with the appropriate settings. On the next Puppet run, Keystone will be reconfigured to use Active Directory for authentication.

As we mentioned before, the method of having Keystone authenticate users against LDAP is being phased out in favor of having the Apache HTTP server perform the authentication itself and then pass through a `REMOTE_USER` environment variable. By default, Packstack will provision Keystone as a **Web Server Gateway Interface** (**WSGI**) service within Apache. Configuring the Keystone virtual host to authenticate users is described at `http://docs.openstack.org/developer/keystone/external-auth.html`.

Provisioning workflows

We've spent almost the entirety of this book discussing how to implement OpenStack and very little of it discussing how most organizations are actually using it. In this section, we'll explore different ways that OpenStack adopters typically provision virtual infrastructure. First, we'll look at giving users access to the Horizon user interface. Then, we'll look at provisioning through the Nova, Cinder, and Neutron APIs. Finally, we'll look at using Heat to orchestrate the OpenStack infrastructure using templates.

The Horizon user interface

The Horizon dashboard UI provides an intuitive and standardized interface for users who already understand the concepts of cloud computing and want to have complete control over their provisioned infrastructure. The dashboard works particularly well in situations where the end user is expected to provide some level of support, where they are responsible for scheduling their own backups, for example. We've seen this approach used in public web hosting companies and also in private cloud use cases where the primary goal is to provide low-cost compute environments to development teams.

Organizations that provide access to the dashboard to their end users will typically customize it to some extent. The appearance of the dashboard is relatively trivial to customize. The Liberty release of OpenStack introduced the concept of **themes** for Horizon, which provides a standardized way of changing colors, images, and layouts. There is also a simple mechanism for enabling or disabling the various panels on the dashboard. Finally, it is also possible to override the Python classes that correspond to the panels by means of a **customization module**. We've seen organizations do this when they want to gather additional information from users when they're provisioning infrastructure. Information on the various options is available at `http://docs.openstack.org/developer/horizon/topics/customizing.html`.

The following screenshot represents the Horizon dashboard UI:

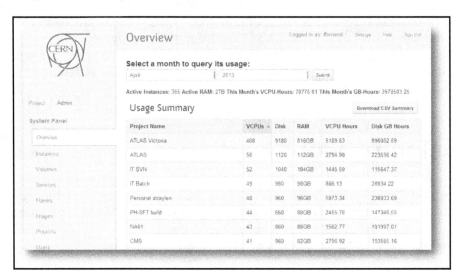

Conseil Européen pour la Recherche Nucléaire (CERN)customized OpenStack dashboard

While creating a custom theme for the Horizon dashboard is relatively simple and is probably a prerequisite for organizations that are going to provide access to their end users, overriding the classes that make up the dashboard is a relatively expensive option to pursue. While the initial development may not be that difficult, it introduces a support burden in the longer term. It also adds additional testing requirements that are difficult to automate. For these reasons, organizations which want to tailor the provisioning process to their specific goals will typically use an external service catalog, which interacts with the API on behalf of the end users.

Using the REST APIs

The OpenStack REST APIs are patterned after the Amazon EC2 APIs and are simple to interact with. There are typically two options for this interaction, depending on the language that the provisioning system is written in. Clients can either call the APIs directly using the language's HTTP or REST library or they can use one of the many **cloud libraries** that have sprung up in the last few years. These libraries can greatly simplify development by taking care of the authentication and serialization pieces of the work, but they can also limit the available API actions. Cloud libraries that we've seen commonly used these days include Apache jclouds for Java, OpenStack Shade for Python, and Fog for Ruby.

In this chapter, we'll interact directly with the REST APIs. Let's breakdown how a virtual instance would be launched using the REST API:

1. The client requests a token from Keystone.
2. The client retrieves a list of keypairs from Nova.
3. The client retrieves a list of images from Nova.
4. The client retrieves a list of flavors from Nova.
5. The client retrieves a list of networks from Neutron.
6. The client optionally creates a volume in Cinder.
7. The client asks Nova to create an instance with the selected image, flavor, network, and (optionally) volume.

The client can then perform various actions on the instance when created, including termination. Let's walk through this workflow using the Python requests library:

1. First, we'll request a token from Keystone (the actual Python code is as follows):

```
import requests #http://docs.python-requests.org/en/latest
import json

KEYSTONE_URL = 'http://controller:5000/v2.0/'
TENANT       = 'demo'
USERNAME     = 'demo'
PASSWORD     = 'secret'

r = requests.post("%s/tokens"% (KEYSTONE_URL,), json={
  "auth": {
    "tenantName": TENANT,
    "passwordCredentials": {
      "username": USERNAME,
      "password": PASSWORD,
    }
```

```
  }
})

if r.ok:
  token = r.json()['access']['token']['id']
else:
  raise Exception(r.text)
```

2. The requests library simplifies working with the REST interface a little by deserializing the JSON returned by Keystone into a Python dictionary via the `json()` function. The response from Keystone contains the token ID, which we will include as a header to any further requests:

```
# Place the token in the X-Auth-Token header
headers = {'X-Auth-Token': token}
```

3. The response from Keystone also contains a service catalog, a set of links to the other services that we want to interact with. Keystone may give out links for more than one region, depending on the configuration. In our lab, though, we can just use the first link for each service. The following code will search the catalog for the compute and network services:

```
# Find the link to the Nova API in the service catalog:
for service in r.json()['access']['serviceCatalog']:
  if service['type'] == 'compute':
    nova_endpoint = service['endpoints'][0]['publicURL']
  if service['type'] == 'network':
    neutron_endpoint = service['endpoints'][0]['publicURL']
```

Note that the endpoint in the catalog is scoped to the tenant we authenticated with. For example, if our tenant ID is 8ce08c9fa6c54ba094be743a55dc5b9a, our Nova endpoint will be http://10.3.71.50:8774/v2/8ce08c9fa6c54ba094be743a55dc5b9a. As such, the only endpoint that shouldn't be dynamically determined is the Keystone endpoint. All other endpoints that need to be interacted with should be pulled from the service catalog.

4. Next, we'll look up the keypair, image, flavor, and network to use when launching the image:

```
keypair_ref = None
# Get the list of available keypairs:
keypairs = requests.get("%s/os-keypairs"% nova_endpoint,
headers=headers)
# take the first one
```

```
keypair_ref = keypairs.json()['keypairs'][0]['keypair']['name']

image_ref = None
# Get the list of available images:
images = requests.get("%s/images"% nova_endpoint,
headers=headers)
# Select the "cirros" image:
for image in images.json()['images']:
  if image['name'] == 'cirros':
    image_ref = image['id']

flavor_ref = None
# Get the list of available flavors:
flavors = requests.get("%s/flavors"% nova_endpoint,
headers=headers)
# Select the "m1.small" flavor
for flavor in flavors.json()['flavors']:
  if flavor['name'] == 'm1.small':
    flavor_ref = flavor['id']

network_ref = None
# Get the list of available networks:
networks = requests.get("%s/v2.0/networks"% neutron_endpoint,
headers=headers)
# Select the "private" network
for network in networks.json()['networks']:
  if network['name'] == 'private':
    network_ref = network['id']
```

Each of these GET requests includes the token that we retrieved from Keystone in the headers. The keypair and flavor are retrieved from the Nova API, as is the image, although it is actually stored in Glance. The network reference is also available from the Nova API, but we retrieve it from the Neutron API in this example. The Neutron API provides more information and control over the network objects.

Note that while the Nova endpoint includes a version string (v2), the Neutron endpoint does not. Also, note that the Neutron endpoint does not include the tenant ID. Each OpenStack API was developed independently by different teams and there is little consistency between them.

5. The following code will launch an instance using the four references we retrieved in the previous section:

```
# Launch the instance:
server = requests.post("%s/servers"% (nova_endpoint,), json={
```

```
      "server": {
        "name": "new_server",
        "imageRef": image_ref,
        "flavorRef": flavor_ref,
        "key_name": keypair_ref,
        "networks": [{
          "uuid": network_ref
        }]
      }
    },
    headers=headers)
    server_ref = server.json()['server']['id']
```

The preceding behavior is normal for REST API; this is a POST request with JSON. There are a couple of things to note about this call. The first is that the call blocks only as long as it takes for the Nova scheduler to accept the request. A successful return code does not mean that the instance was successfully launched. The second is that the JSON returned by the API is not a serialized representation of the server object. Instead, it provides a set of links to the representation of the object. The link to the object comprises the API version, the tenant ID, the string servers, and the instance ID. For example, http://192.168.0.10:8774/v2/8ce08c9fa6c54ba094be743a55dc5b9a/servers/d87f6e9d-347e-48f3-acfb-6f2e85c43629.
The following request provides the status of the instance:

```
requests.get(server.json()['server']['links'][0]['href'],
headers=headers)
```

6. Once an instance has been created, actions can be POSTed to the instance's URL with the string action appended. For example, the following code will stop an instance:

```
server_url = server.json()['server']['links'][0]['href']
stop = requests.post("%s/action"% (server_url,), json={
  "os-stop": None
}, headers=headers)
```

7. Finally, to delete an instance, issue an HTTP DELETE request to the server's URL:

```
delete = requests.delete(server_url, headers=headers)
```

As with any of the request responses in this example, the HTTP status code indicates the success or failure of the request. The successful status code for the delete request is 204 and the successful status code for an action is typically 202. More information on expected status codes, request parameters, and response parameters is available in the Compute API documentation at http://developer.openstack.org/api-ref-compute-v2.1.html.

Provisioning with templates

The end users of the service catalogs that drive the provisioning workflows for software-defined infrastructures tend to be application developers. Allowing developers to provision networks, volumes, and instances via APIs is extremely useful for automated continuous integration builds and deployments. Though there are a number of advantages to this approach, many organizations would prefer to let their developers provision environments made up of these elements instead. First off, the number of options exposed either in the API or in the Horizon dashboard is pretty impressive. A typical deployment will have at least two or three flavors, four or five images, private and public networks, arbitrary volume sizes, and so on. Choosing from all of these options to just launch an instance is time-consuming. It can also put a burden on the team that has to support them. Once software-defined networking is introduced, the end user may be expected to understand networking, routing, and load balancing in order to provision a working system. This is really unrealistic in most enterprise environments.

The solution to managing the complexity of software-defined infrastructure is to compose a service catalog of templates. These templates can be made up of single instances or multiple instances, rich or simple network topologies, and highly customized or standard images.

The orchestration API is much simpler to program to as well. Let's walk through an example:

1. We begin the same way as the previous example, by requesting a token from Keystone:

```
import requests #http://docs.python-requests.org/en/latest
import json

KEYSTONE_URL = 'http://controller01:5000/v2.0/'
TENANT      = 'demo'
USERNAME    = 'demo'
PASSWORD    = 'secret'

r = requests.post("%s/tokens"% (KEYSTONE_URL,), json={
  "auth": {
    "tenantName": TENANT,
```

```
        "passwordCredentials": {
          "username": USERNAME,
          "password": PASSWORD,
        }
      }
    })

    if r.ok:
      token = r.json()['access']['token']['id']
    else:
      raise Exception(r.text)

    # Place the token in the X-Auth-Token header
    headers = {'X-Auth-Token': token}
```

2. Then, instead of searching for the Compute API, we'll search for the endpoint of the Orchestration service:

```
    # Find the link to the Heat API in the service catalog:
    for service in r.json()['access']['serviceCatalog']:
      if service['type'] == 'orchestration':
        heat_endpoint = service['endpoints'][0]['publicURL']
```

The Heat URL, like the Nova URL, contains the UUID of the tenant.

3. Finally, we POST the JSON string representing the Heat template to the service:

```
    stack = requests.post("%s/stacks"% (heat_endpoint,), json={
      "stack_name": "new_server",
      "template": {
        "heat_template_version": "2013-05-23",
        "resources": {
          "new_server_port": {
            "type": "OS::Neutron::Port",
            "properties": {
              "network": "private"
            }
          },
          "new_server": {
            "type": "OS::Nova::Server",
            "properties": {
              "key_name": "demo",
              "flavor": "m1.small",
              "image": "cirros",
              "networks": [ {
                "port": {
                  "get_resource": "new_server_port"
                }
```

```
        } ]
      }
    }
  }
}
}, headers=headers)
```

Heat performs the name-to-ID translations for us, so we don't need to look up the reference for the flavor, image, key, or network. The response to the call contains the status code (201 is success) and a link to the (stack.json()['stack']['links'][0]['href']) stack object. The Heat API exposes an `actions` link similar to the Compute API. Stacks may be suspended and resumed via that mechanism.

Perhaps the most important feature of the Heat API, though, is the ability to reference an external template. To use this feature, use the `template_url` attribute instead of specifying a template. Observe the following example:

```
stack = requests.post("%s/stacks"% (heat_endpoint,), json={
  "stack_name": "new_server",
  "template_url": "http://www.example.com/heat-
  templates/new_server.yaml"
}, headers=headers)
```

The templates can then be separated from the provisioning code. This allows them to reside in separate version control repositories and allows different teams to work on the catalog and the provisioning logic out of step.

Almost every object that can be created via the OpenStack APIs can be orchestrated using Heat. For more information on heat templates, refer to the Heat Template Guide at `http ://docs.openstack.org/developer/heat/template_guide/`.

Metering and billing

Whether you're building a public cloud or a private cloud, one of the most critical capabilities of the system is tracking the usage of the virtual objects that are provisioned by the users or tenants. Usage in OpenStack is tracked largely in the same way it is in Amazon Web Services. For compute resources, the system tracks when a particular instance was started and when it was terminated. The cost of a compute resource is associated with the number of CPU cores or the amount of memory in the flavor associated with the instance. Some organizations may also associate a cost with the image as well.

For example, an instantiation of a Red Hat Enterprise Linux image may cost a certain number of cents per hour, whereas an instantiation of a Microsoft Windows image may cost something different. Other resources may be billed based on when they're provisioned regardless of use. For example, a tenant might be charged for how long a floating IP was assigned to the project, regardless of whether it was attached to an instance. Cinder volumes are frequently treated this way.

Whether your organization intends to charge your customers based on consumption or your organization intends to just show your customers their consumption, there are a few different strategies for tracking and reporting usage data. Some organizations that provision resources onto OpenStack via the API by a service catalog choose to use the service catalog implementation as the system of record. This helps maintain consistency for the user. For example, if they've provisioned a three tier-application, they probably want to be billed for a three-tier application and not for three virtual machines, a Cinder volume, and a floating IP. For PaaS or Continuous Integration use cases, though, the total amount of compute and storage used over a period of time is probably more important.

There are a few basic approaches to tracking usage in OpenStack. Systems can listen for events on the message bus or query Ceilometer for them and then extrapolate usage data. Systems can also query Ceilometer directly for usage data. Each of these approaches is also useful for other use cases than metering and billing and some are better suited than others for each of them. For example, listening and timing events can offer great insights into the performance of a system. Also, compliance workflows may be driven by certain events within the OpenStack system.

Listening to OpenStack

There are two modes of internal communication in the OpenStack system. The first is to GET or POST to the REST API and the second is to pull and push messages onto the message queue. Each of the services uses a combination of each; when the Nova API gets a request to provision a resource over the REST API, it passes that request along to the compute nodes via the message bus. They send back usage data over the bus, but they use the API to communicate with other services. These two modes of communication are also available for integration. Just as we can provision resources using the REST API, we can track their progress using the message bus.

The following code example uses the Kombu library in Python to attach to the Nova queue on the message bus to listen for these RPC calls between the various Nova services. First, we define a callback method to be used to process events on the bus. This simple method just prints the body of the message:

```
from kombu import Connection, Exchange, Queue

def process_message(body, message):
    print body
    message.ack()
```

Then we create a queue named `listener` and bind it to the `nova` exchange. In the following example, we're going to subscribe to all messages on the `nova` queue:

```
nova_exchange = Exchange('nova', 'topic', durable=False)
nova_queue    = Queue('listener', exchange = nova_exchange,
routing_key='#')
conn = Connection('amqp://guest:guest@192.168.0.10//')
consumer = conn.Consumer(nova_queue, callbacks=[process_message])
consumer.consume()
```

 Note that the `connection` string is specific to the deployment in question. The username and password for the message bus should align with the settings in `/etc/nova/nova.conf`.

Finally, we'll check the queue for messages and process them:

```
while True:
    conn.drain_events()
```

Running this example will show just how chatty the Nova services are. The message format for these RPC messages is well defined, but the content of the messages is version-specific. For these reasons, most developers will choose to use the notification subsystem instead.

Using the notification subsystem

Each of the OpenStack services can be configured to emit notifications on the message bus. These notifications can then be picked up by messaging clients or by the Ceilometer service. Notifications were originally implemented by each service separately, but the functionality has been folded into the Oslo Messaging library as a common interface.

To enable notification in Nova, the following settings need to be changed in `/etc/nova/nova.conf`:

nova.conf Setting	Example value	Description
`instance_usage_audit`	`true`	Turns on usage auditing
`instance_usage_audit_period`	`hour`	Sets usage auditing to hourly
`notify_on_state_change`	`vm_and_task_state`	Tells Nova to send a notification when a VM's state changes
`notification_driver`	`messagingv2`	Tells Nova to send notifications to the message bus

Other notification drivers are available as well. Notifications can be sent to syslog, for example. For more information, refer to the Oslo Messaging FAQ at `http://docs.openstack.org/developer/oslo.messaging/FAQ.html`.

A simple client that can listen to these Notification events is provided here:

```python
#!/usr/bin/env python

from kombu import Connection, Exchange, Queue

def process_message(body, message):
  print body
  message.ack()

nova_exchange = Exchange('nova', 'topic', durable=False)
notifications_queue    = Queue('notification-listener', exchange =
nova_exchange, routing_key='notifications.info')
conn = Connection('amqp://guest:guest@192.168.0.10//')
consumer = conn.Consumer(notifications_queue, callbacks=[process_message])
consumer.consume()

while True:
  conn.drain_events()
```

This example creates a queue named `notification-listener`, which is bound to the `nova` exchange. Instead of listening to all events on the exchange, though, we subscribe to the `notifications.info` topic. This ensures that we receive only the messages that are designated as notifications by the Nova service.

A higher level abstraction, which can be used by Python programmers who are interacting with OpenStack, can be found in the `oslo.messaging` library. Documentation on this approach is available at `http://docs.openstack.org/developer/oslo.messaging/notification_listener.html`. Another option is to use the Yagi library (`https://github.com/rackerlabs/yagi`), which is in turn used by Stack Tach from Rackspace (`https://github.com/openstack/stacktach`).

Consuming events from Ceilometer

Consuming events from the message queue allows for a push-style integration model in the OpenStack environment. Writing and maintaining a daemon to consume events from the queue and act on them can be onerous for many organizations, though. A much simpler option is to poll the Ceilometer interface for events over the REST API. Given that Nova (as well as other services) is configured to emit notifications over the message bus, the Ceilometer service can store them and make them available for polling. To enable this functionality, set `store_events` to `True` in `/etc/ceilometer/ceilometer.conf`.

The following example shows how to retrieve events from Ceilometer using the Python requests library:

1. First, we begin by retrieving a token from Keystone:

```
import requests #http://docs.python-requests.org/en/latest
import json

KEYSTONE_URL = 'http://controller01:5000/v2.0/'
TENANT       = 'demo'
USERNAME     = 'demo'
PASSWORD     = 'secret'

r = requests.post("%s/tokens"% (KEYSTONE_URL,), json={
  "auth": {
    "tenantName": TENANT,
    "passwordCredentials": {
      "username": USERNAME,
      "password": PASSWORD,
    }
  }
})
if r.ok:
  token = r.json()['access']['token']['id']
else:
  raise Exception(r.text)
```

```
# Place the token in the X-Auth-Token header
headers = {'X-Auth-Token': token}
```

2. Then we find the `metering` service in Keystone's catalog:

```
# Find the link to the Ceilometer API in the service catalog:
for service in r.json()['access']['serviceCatalog']:
    if service['type'] == 'metering':
        metering_endpoint = service['endpoints'][0]['publicURL']
```

3. Finally, we request all available events using a GET request and print out the types:

```
events = requests.get("%s/v2/events"% (metering_endpoint,),
headers=headers)

for e in events.json():
    print e['event_type']
```

The GET request can contain filters for certain types of event and can contain a limit to the number of events to retrieve. For more information on using the Ceilometer Event API, refer to `http://docs.openstack.org/developer/ceilometer/webapi/v2.html`.

Reading meters in Ceilometer

In the preceding sections, we've walked through different methods for retrieving event data from an OpenStack cloud. This event data can then be used to track usage and generate billing information for end users of the system. The Ceilometer service was designed to do exactly that; track usage based on event data and generate billing information. Ceilometer makes this data available via a REST API.

The following example uses the Python requests library to request the duration of instances running within the user's tenant:

1. First, we begin by requesting a token from Keystone:

```
#!/usr/bin/env python

import requests #http://docs.python-requests.org/en/latest
import json

KEYSTONE_URL = 'http://controller01:5000/v2.0/'
TENANT       = 'demo'
USERNAME     = 'demo'
PASSWORD     = 'secret'
```

```
r = requests.post("%s/tokens"% (KEYSTONE_URL,), json={
  "auth": {
    "tenantName": TENANT,
    "passwordCredentials": {
      "username": USERNAME,
      "password": PASSWORD,
    }
  }
})

if r.ok:
  token = r.json()['access']['token']['id']
else:
  raise Exception(r.text)

# Place the token in the X-Auth-Token header
headers = {'X-Auth-Token': token}
```

2. Then, we get the link to the Ceilometer service from the service catalog:

```
# Find the link to the Ceilometer API in the service catalog:
for service in r.json()['access']['serviceCatalog']:
  if service['type'] == 'metering':
    metering_endpoint = service['endpoints'][0]['publicURL']
```

3. Next, we issue a GET request for the statistics for the `Meter` instance. Ceilometer comes with a set of predefined meters for things such as instance run time, CPU usage, disk usage, and so on:

```
tenant_id = r.json()['access']['token']['tenant']['id']
filter = {'q.field': 'project', 'q.value': tenant_id}
statistics = requests.get("%s/v2/meters/instance/statistics"%
(metering_endpoint,), headers=headers)
```

For a full list of available meters, refer to `http://docs.openstack.org/admin-guide-clou d/telemetry-measurements.html`.

> Notice that we've scoped the request for statistics to our own tenant with a search filter. A call which generates a billing statement for each tenant would iterate through the list of tenants and gather the usage for each of them. It would also be scoped to a period of time with an additional filter. More information on filters is available at `http://docs.openstack.org/d eveloper/ceilometer/webapi/v2.html`.

The JSON returned by the call contains a list of statistics. We're interested in the `duration` value:

```
print statistics.json()[0]['duration']
```

Other statistics are available for meters such as `sums`, `averages`, `minimums`, and `maximums`.

Updating the design document

In this chapter, we've identified several different ways to interact with OpenStack using the available APIs. Now is a good time to revisit the design document and fill out the **Requirements** section. An ideal set of requirements for an OpenStack cloud will have the following characteristics:

- Each requirement should be atomic to limit the scope of the requirement
- Each requirement should contain context; there should be information on who will be using the functionality and under what circumstances
- Each requirement should be testable, ideally in an automated fashion

If these conditions are met, we can generate policy documentation based on which roles should have access to which functionality and we can generate automated test suites that verify that the requirements of the platform are met. These test suites can in turn be used in monitoring suites to ensure that the running system is performing according to specification.

Writing requirements

In this section, we'll look at some example requirements. As we saw earlier in the chapter, every interaction with the OpenStack REST APIs starts with a request to Keystone for a token. The following user story is a good representation of that interaction:

"As an End User of the system, I should be able to present my Active Directory username and password to the Keystone service and receive a token which authorizes me to use other OpenStack services. This token will be scoped to the projects to which I have been granted access by the OpenStack Administrator."

The following metadata can be associated with this requirement:

- **User**: End user
- **Inputs**: Active Directory authentication credentials
- **Outputs**: Authorization token and Project scope

We can then also describe an implementation of the requirement using the REST API:

```
POST /v2.0/tokens
{
   "auth": {
     "tenantName": "demo",
     "passwordCredentials": {
        "username": "demo",
        "password": "secret"
     }
   }
}
RESPONSE 200
{
   "access": {
     "token": {
        "issued_at": "2014-01-30T15:30:58.819584",
        "expires": "2014-01-31T15:30:58Z",
        "id": "aaaaa-bbbbb-ccccc-dddd",
        "tenant": {
          "description": null,
          "enabled": true,
          "id": "fc394f2ab2df4114bde39905f800dc57",
          "name": "demo"
        }
     },
   }
}
```

If we wanted to, we could also identify the service level agreement for this requirement. For example, we could specify that the `Keystone` service should respond within 10 seconds with a valid token. This could be used to establish acceptable performance thresholds for the system.

Let's walk through a more complex example, that of launching an instance:

> *"As an End User of the system, I should be able to present my Keystone token and instantiate a given image as a virtual machine via the Nova API. I should be able to specify the image, the flavor, an SSH key, a private network, and metadata for the instance."*

The following metadata can be associated with this requirement:

- **User**: End user
- **Inputs**: Keystone token, compute service API, tenant ID, image ID, flavor ID, SSH key name, network ID, and metadata keys and values
- **Outputs**: Instance description

An example of this requirement is as follows:

```
POST /v2.1/{tenant_id}/servers
{
   "server": {
     "name": "example-server",
     "imageRef": "{image_id}",
     "flavorRef": "{flavor_id}",
     "key_name": "{key_name}"
     "networks": "{"uuid": "{network_id}"}"
     "metadata": {
        "{metadata_key}": "{metadata_value}"
     }
   }
}
RESPONSE 202
{
   "server": {
     "id": "{server_id}",
     "links": [
     {
        "href": "/v2.1/{tenant_id}/servers/{server_id}",
        "rel": "self"
     },
     {
        "href": "/servers/{server_id}",
        "rel": "bookmark"
     }
     ],
   }
}
```

Notice that we've kept the requirement relatively simple. We could have walked through the whole call and response script leading up to the final call, but that's really better served in the test implementation. We'll walk through how to translate requirements into tests in the next section.

Testing requirements

In Chapter 4, *Building the Deployment Pipeline*, we wrote some basic tests for our OpenStack deployment using shell tools. In this section, we'll combine the code examples discussed earlier in the chapter with the Python unittest library to generate a set of automated tests that can be run from Jenkins to verify our deployment. The following example, which uses the Python unittest and requests libraries, is very simple, but can be used as a starting point:

```python
#!/usr/bin/env python

import unittest
import requests #http://docs.python-requests.org/en/latest
import json

KEYSTONE_URL = 'http://controller01:5000/v2.0/'
TENANT       = 'demo'
USERNAME     = 'demo'
PASSWORD     = 'secret'
```

Once we've imported the necessary libraries and set the global variables, we'll create a TestCase object for our tests:

```python
class TestKeystone(unittest.TestCase):
"""Set of Keystone-specific tests"""
```

Any function whose name begins with test will be treated as a test to be run by the unittest library. We'll define a function that exercises the REST call described in the first user story:

```python
def test_001_get_token(self):
"""Requirement 001: Authorization Token"""
r = requests.post("%s/tokens"% (KEYSTONE_URL,), json={
  "auth": {
    "tenantName": TENANT,
    "passwordCredentials": {
      "username": USERNAME,
      "password": PASSWORD,
    }
  }
```

```
  })
  if r.ok:
     self.assertEqual(r.status_code, 200)
     token = r.json()['access']['token']['id']
     self.assertTrue(token)
  else:
     raise Exception(r.text)
```

This test is based on the examples that we used earlier in this chapter to retrieve a token from the `Keystone` service. We've added two assertion statements that verify the service is responding the way we've designed it. The first asserts that the response code is `200` and the second asserts that the JSON response contains a value for the token.

To enable the test to be run from the command line, we add a call to the `unittest` library at the end of the script:

```
  if __name__ == '__main__':
     unittest.main()
```

If we check this script into the `test` directory of the code repository we created in Chapter 4, *Building the Deployment Pipeline*, we can call this automated test by running the script from Jenkins. Each requirement in the design document should have an automated test associated with it in this fashion. As requirements are added to the design document and implemented in Puppet, new tests that represent them can be added to the suite.

Summary

In this chapter, we've looked at three integration patterns within the OpenStack platform. The first pattern was to use the built-in integration functionality provided by Keystone to integrate with Active Directory. The second was to use the REST APIs to provision infrastructure into the OpenStack environment. The third was to listen in on the message bus for notifications. Once we had explored the various ways that we can interact with the system, we wrote requirements for our deployed system in the design document with them in mind. Finally, these requirements were translated into automated tests that could be inserted into the deployment pipeline.

Some of the organizations that we've worked with have expressed frustration at the complexity of integrating the OpenStack platform with the other services in their environment. For these organizations, a **Cloud Management Platform** (**CMP**) that obfuscates some of the technical details of integration is an option worth considering. CMPs such as Red Hat's CloudForms or Dell's Cloud Manager will wire into the REST APIs and the message bus of an OpenStack implementation and allow for higher-level access to the objects within the virtual infrastructure. They also offer out-of-the-box integrations with third-party authentication, service catalogs, and billing systems.

We like to think of the entire OpenStack system as a massive integration platform. Before OpenStack, organizations spent huge amounts of resources integrating their storage, network and compute infrastructure with their organizational infrastructure. The open design of the system is one of its greatest strengths. In the next chapter, we will be discussing OpenStack security. We will examine common security practices such as logging, patching, and encryption as well as some application security suggestions.

References

- Keystone is not an authentication service, Nathan Kinder: `https://blog-nkinde r.rhcloud.com/?p=130`
- How to Integrate Keystone with Active Directory: `https://wiki.openstack.org /wiki/HowtoIntegrateKeystonewithAD`
- Customizing Horizon: `http://docs.openstack.org/developer/horizon/topic s/customizing.html`
- OpenStack API Documentation: `http://developer.openstack.org/api-guide /quick-start/index.html`

7
Securing the Cloud

As more companies begin to bring OpenStack out of the development environments and into production (refer to the following chart), real concerns about security are beginning to take priority. This chapter will not only help outline some best practices about the OpenStack infrastructure security, but also highlight how OpenStack users and operators can bring the same level of legacy security to workloads that run on top of OpenStack clouds:

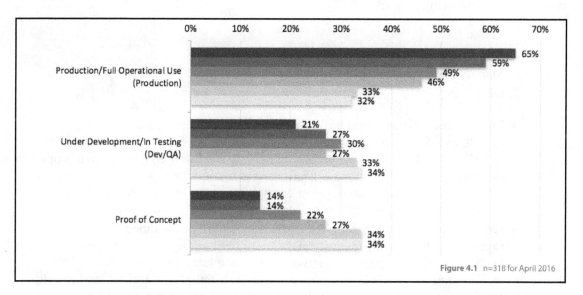

Figure 4.1 n=318 for April 2016

Security zones within OpenStack

Within an OpenStack deployment exists a series of logical security zones. These are the basic areas of trust within the OpenStack platform that can be leveraged by applications, servers, networks, or users. These zones have an increasing level of trust and can be broken down into the following zones:

1. Public
2. Guest
3. Management
4. Data

- **Public zones**: These zones within OpenStack are an entirely untrusted area of any cloud infrastructure. By convention, they are the most open and are thus called public. They are not necessarily open to the Internet, but the area is open to being consumed by untrusted resources and on networks without the operators direct authority. This area requires encryption and other compensating controls in order to meet the security requirements of most organizations.

- **Guest zones**: These zones are for instances that are provisioned within the OpenStack cloud. They include inter-tenant network instance traffic (one instance to another across segregated networks or on the same tenant network). This traffic is not the traffic that supports the infrastructure of the cloud and provides the API access to OpenStacks native RESTful API endpoints. Providing unregulated public IP addresses into instances that reside in this domain will cause the domain to be untrusted. The only way this area can be considered trusted is when the compensating controls have been implemented to regulate public IP access into this zone using external network controls.

- **Management zones**: These are the zones where the OpenStack services reside and interact. These particular zones are typically isolated for OpenStack control plane traffic only. Due to the sensitive nature of this internal communication, steps must be taken to harden this particular network, and access to this network should only be given to the servers that are operating the control plane for OpenStack. Once this is done, this zone is considered trusted. In any case where this zone is made to be routed or connected to a routable network, in effect bridging it to an untrusted zone, this network immediately becomes untrusted and must have compensating controls implemented immediately.

- **Data zones**: These are the security zones that primarily contain the services and network traffic pertaining to the storage services within OpenStack. This data typically requires high security and high levels of confidentiality. The level of trust in this network zone is highly dependent on the workloads running in the cloud and the type of deployment that is done. Therefore, this zone can be trusted or untrusted, and without knowing the specifics of the type of deployment we cannot assign a default level of trust. It is important to understand these zones when considering OpenStack security and the resources and services running on the platform. Developers have purposely segregated access to varying parts of the platform to segregate privileged and nonprivileged zones as well as to reduce cross-zone attacks.

Software vulnerabilities

OpenStack is an orchestration platform written mostly in Python that runs on top of a Linux-based operating system. This orchestration platform is responsible for provisioning instances or Infrastructure as a service to tenants in support of workloads that are required to run in a cloud environment. Therefore, OpenStack software vulnerabilities can be broken down into two main groups. The first group consists of instances or bare metal servers that OpenStack provisions and orchestrates, the second consists of the OpenStack infrastructure environment and its hosts.

Instance software security and patching

Under OpenStack, the hypervisor creates and runs independent virtual machines or instances. These instances require software updates and patching separate from the underlying OpenStack infrastructure on which it resides. Updates to the hypervisor and underlying server operating systems are not propagated up to the active workloads and instances; therefore, two strategies must exist-one for instances running on the cloud and another for the cloud infrastructure.

The instance strategy should align with the existing organizational and governance policies that are currently in effect that control patching of existing legacy systems. Since OpenStack launches instances based on images and flavors that may have executable metadata injected into the instance upon boot, there are multiple ways to ensure the latest hardened image is used prior to launching an instance depending on the workload type.

For the traditional, ephemeral workloads commonly found on OpenStack clouds, regular updates to the Glance images should be performed as per organizational policy and should be controlled by a trusted organization within a company. These updates should add patches and security fixes to an operating system and be imported as an existing image in the glance repository. These updated images should be tested in a lower development or sandbox environment before implementing into production. These updated images will then serve as the base operating system for any new instances using that image as well as ephemeral workloads that, have been using that image. However, the running image will not change. The security patches will not take effect until the instances are rebooted. Typically, ephemeral workloads tend to be able to reboot without impact to the availability of the application, however, persistent workloads running on the cloud will need to develop application based strategies for maintaining uptime of the application while patching. Some organizations have strict rules about reboots of instances running on old versions of images depending on whether the patch applied to the image was for security or simply an update.

Default OpenStack security policies should be created to allow legacy software compliance tools to scan hosts for software update compliance. In the case of persistent workloads and instances not experiencing frequent reboots or that need to maintain certain levels of availability, security policies may be created to allow these instances to use legacy software repository based patching solutions and implement patches in a traditional fashion by patching the running instance. However, there may be additional network configurations needed to make the software repositories available within tenant networks based on an organization's OpenStack network deployment. For both the ephemeral and persistent workloads, cloud-init and cloudbase-init could be used to execute an update to an image upon boot using native software management tools and the local software repositories. However, these updates that would occur upon boot may delay provisioning depending on the number of updates performed on the image. This is why the updating of the base glance images is the best practice for security and software update compliance of instances.

Infrastructure host security and patching

Security is a fundamental part of the OpenStack architecture and needs to be maintained in order to protect the various security zones of the stack. OpenStack is a complex platform comprised of many different parts that are actively and continually being developed by multiple different parties. On the surface, this can seem fundamentally insecure, however, not only is OpenStack being developed by thousands of individuals, it is also being tested and scrutinized by thousands of users and developers. These users and developers create a useful feedback loop to other developers and testers. This provides almost constant vigilance against sloppy and insecure code. However, as in commercial software, security issues have still been discovered. This is why the OpenStack Foundation has created an OpenStack Security Team that publishes advisories about identified security issues, descriptions, and links to patches.

Patching OpenStack code

These patches are for vulnerabilities in the code for OpenStack. The current security advisory list is maintained at `https://security.openstack.org/ossalist.html`, where patches are also provided. These patches are mostly upgraded Python files that can simply replace the existing file on the OpenStack control or compute servers. An example of a patch that includes replacement files for a bug discovered in the neutron can be seen at `https://review.openstack.org/#/c/299025/`. The OpenStack Vulnerability Management Team is responsible for the bug and fix process for security and OpenStack at `https://wiki.openstack.org/wiki/Vulnerability_Management`.

Patching the operating system

A much larger part of the platform is the underlying operating system and/or tools. Since OpenStack can support many different hypervisors and run on multiple platforms, we will concentrate our discussion on Linux. The Linux distributions that are most commonly seen running OpenStack are represented in the following chart, taken at the most recent OpenStack Summit (https://www.openstack.org/assets/survey/April-2016-User-Survey-Report.pdf):

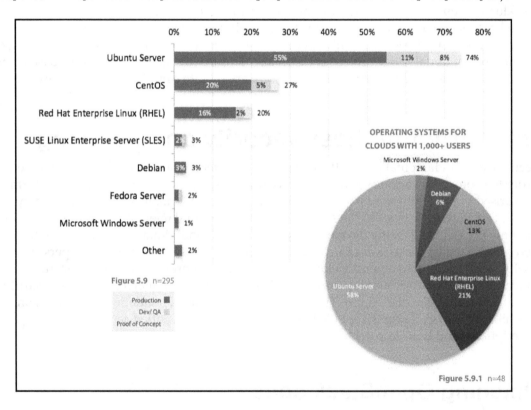

Figure 5.9 n=295

Figure 5.9.1 n=48

As the chart clearly shows, Ubuntu, CentOS, and Red Hat Enterprise Linux are the top three operating systems powering OpenStack today. Not surprisingly, two of these three distributions, Red Hat and Canonical (Ubuntu) are heavily involved with OpenStack development community and the third distribution is not a commercial release, rather it is the Community Development Platform for the Red Hat family of Linux distributions (https://wiki.centos.org/FAQ/General). Therefore, CentOS is included with these, developing OpenStack to run on Red Hat distributions. CentOS typically releases bug fixes for OS issues within 72 hours of Red Hat delivering a new package.

Red Hat Enterprise Linux and CentOS

Using any distribution of Linux, it is vital to update any affected software in a timely manner to limit security risks. If the software is part of a package within Red Hat, the vulnerability should be patched as soon as it is released by Red Hat. Often, Red Hat includes patches with their security announcements and then releases it as a security erratum update. Again, it is vital to apply patches and updates as soon as they are released to help eliminate the risk of an attacker using the bug against your OpenStack infrastructure. This can be accomplished using the Yum Package Manager to download from only trusted sources. These trusted sources could be the **Red Hat Network (RHN)** or a local repository that is under your organization's control. All downloaded packages from outside your organization should be verified for authenticity using the GNU Privacy Guard or GNUPG, a free package used for ensuring the authenticity of package files. If the verification fails, either the package is corrupt or it has been compromised.

Canonical Ubuntu based operating systems

The Ubuntu security and patching ecosystem is very similar to Red Hat. Security updates are released by Canonical's Ubuntu developers whenever they discover and patch vulnerabilities. Security notices can be delivered via e-mail or by subscribing via RSS. Ubuntu allows you to have security updates automatically installed – once configured you don't need to run security updates manually again. Ubuntu allows users to configure automatic security updates via `unattended-upgrades` using `cron-apt`. Similar behavior can be applied to Red Hat hosts using `yum-cron` with `update_cmd = minimal-security-severity:Important`.

Software repository management

Software repository management is vital in order to provide secure updates to an OpenStack infrastructure. Red Hat has developed a management application called **Satellite** and Ubuntu has **Landscape**. Both of these are systems management applications that allow administrators to deploy, patch, manage, and monitor their respective systems. These applications are an on-premise way to download and manage content from remote distribution portals. They reduce the amount of traffic over a corporate WAN during system updates, since all packages are only transferred to the local repository once. These applications also manage the update files locally to limit security risks of outside malicious content.

Satellite can even be configured as a single system or as a series of remote systems that act like proxies and get authorization and subscription information from a central server. These commercial applications also give users a single pane of glass for package management and allow profiles of updates to be created for separate classes of servers in the enterprise.

One alternative is to create and maintain a package repository manually using open source tools such as Puppet, Chef, and Ansible by creating scripts that do replication and validation. However, a more complete option is to use a community project such as Pulp (`http://www.pulpproject.org/`). Pulp is a free and open-source platform for managing software repositories. It is configurable to support RPM package types (`rpm`, `srpm`, `errata`, and so on), Puppet modules, Docker images, Atomic Trees, Python packages, and more. There is also a way to support Debian packages through a plugin. With Pulp you can do the following:

- Pull in content from distribution repositories to the Pulp server manually on either a one-time-only or recurring basis
- Upload your own content to the Pulp server (OpenStack security patches)
- Publish content as a web-based repository, a series of ISOs, or various other methods

Software patching and repository management get incrementally more difficult as the number of hosts to be patched increases. Starting an OpenStack deployment with a proper patching strategy and the tools to manage and enable patching is critical for scaling an OpenStack cloud. By applying and testing security patches to the OpenStack infrastructure, first in lower environments and then in production, organizations will ensure that both the development and production environments are secure and tested for operations.

Hardening hypervisors

The Nova service, one of OpenStack's most complex projects, provides compute functionality in the environment. Nova is very pervasive throughout an OpenStack cloud and interacts with most of the other core IaaS services. Proper configuration of this particular service is an important factor in securing an OpenStack deployment.

Standard Linux hardening practices and hypervisors

The key to security in an OpenStack environment is the configuration and hardening of the virtualization technology, also called the hypervisor. While OpenStack can be configured to use many different hypervisors, by far the most common hypervisor in use is KVM. All of the top operating systems such as RHEL, Ubuntu, and CentOS support the KVM hypervisor. All of the top OpenStack distributions such as Red Hat OpenStack Platform, Mirantis OpenStack, and HP Helion use KVM as the default hypervisor. Therefore, we will focus our attention on the KVM hypervisor running on Linux for production grade security.

Additionally, the KVM hypervisor has been certified through the U.S. Government's Common Criteria program on commercial distributions and has been validated to separate the runtime environment of the instances from each other, providing adequate instance separation. For more information refer to `https://www.niap-ccevs.org/NIAP_Evolution /faqs/nstissp-11/`.

Red Hat OpenStack Platform, one distribution that has been Common Criteria certified, had to satisfy the following list of minimal authentication requirements:

- Audit (ability to audit large amounts of events in detail)
- Discretionary access control
- Mandatory access control
- Role-based access control
- Object reuse (file system objects, memory, and IPC objects)
- Security management of administrative users
- Secure communication (SSH)
- Storage encryption (encrypted block device support)
- TSF protection (kernel software and data protection by hardware)

While these identity and authentication functions are required for U.S. Government software certification, these are also essential for production cloud environments, especially those operating in the public zone and connected to the Internet. The output from these tools should be fed into a larger logging, monitoring, and alerting framework that was discussed in Chapter 5, *Building to Operate*. While using tools such as ELK and other log processing and auditing tools, security alerts can be generated when any security event occurs or thresholds are breached.

In addition to identity and authentication, many different cryptographic standards are available to OpenStack for identification, authentication, data transfer encryption, and protection for data at rest. Some of these are as follows:

- AES: Data in motion and data at rest
- TDES: Data in motion
- RSA: Data in motion and identification/authentication
- DSA: Data in motion and identification/authentication
- Serpent: Data at rest
- Twofish: Data at rest
- SHA-1: Data in motion and data at rest
- SHA-2: Data at rest and identification/authorization

It's not only the underlying operating system that must provide features to have optimal security, the hardware that runs the compute host, and thus, the hypervisor should also support the following:

Feature	Hardware Description	Security Enhancement
VT-d / AMD-Vi	I/O MMU	PCI-Passthrough Protection
Intel TXT / SEM	Intel Trusted Execution Technology	Dynamic attestation services
SR-IOV, MR-IOV, ATS	PCI-SIG I/O virtualization	Secure sharing of PCI Express devices by multiple instances.
VT-C	Network Virtualization	Network I/O Improvements on hypervisors

In addition to hardware and operating system requirements, KVM also supports additional features such as sVirt (SELinux and Virtualization), Intel TXT, and AppArmor.

SELinux and AppArmor

At the heart of hypervisor security lies SELinux. SELinux is a labeling system where everything on the system receives a label that SELinux understands and can use for its policy sets. In most default configurations, it comes with multiple policy sets that define how processes with certain labels can interact with processes, files, directories, and so on, that have different labels. This access is enforced by the kernel and the configuration is extremely granular. Unfortunately, some find the configuration very challenging to understand and implement. However, most common adjustments are done via Booleans to toggle access on and off. For example, if a remote server wants to talk to SSHD locally, a single Boolean enables that access.

KVM provides excellent instance isolation through its standard use of MAC policies. This means all instances run as processes and they are confined using SELinux policies. Additionally, KVM has an API for sVirt that ensures that all processes related to a specific instance can only access and manipulate files and devices that are related to that instance. If an attacker were able to find a way to "break out" of the running instance, they would not get full interactive access to the underlying compute node's operating system. The attacker would instead be limited to only those files the instance had access to based on SELinux policies.

On the other hand, AppArmor does not use labels such as SElinux, but instead relies on a set of policy files that specify what to protect. This is accomplished by specifying a particular executable and what it is actually permitted to do. Policies are typically created for binaries such as `/usr/sbin/mysql` or `/sbin/dhclient` and include the ability to include different pluggable configurations for services such as `mysql` and `nameservice`. Capabilities are also configured in AppArmor to override certain default behaviors. However, the bulk of the policy will contain a list of files, directories, and so on and the behaviors that are permitted. For example, an AppArmor profile for MySQL would need to specify read access to the MySQL configuration files. This would be accomplished by adding the following to the policy file for MySQL:

- `/etc/mysql/conf.d/ r`
- `/etc/mysql/conf.d/* r`
- `/etc/mysql/*.cnf r`

These configuration parameters allow the MySQL binary to read the configuration files listed earlier. This behavior and configuration are very similar to Oracle's Trusted Solaris.

Systems running RHEL- and CentOS-based operating systems will see SELinux installed and in an "enforcing" state by default. AppArmor is included with most Debian-based systems including Ubuntu, however, the default behavior of enforcing or complaining varies by version. AppArmor can also be used with the LXD (linux container) hypervisor that Canonical uses in its OpenStack platform distribution.

sVirt

sVirt is a solution that adds effective separation to virtualized environments using **Mandatory Access Control** (**MAC**) with implementations such as SELinux and AppArmor. This hardens systems against bugs in the hypervisor that could be used as an attack vector towards the hypervisor host or another instance running on the same hypervisor. SELinux uses a pluggable framework using MAC and allows guests and their resources to have unique labels. Once all of the instances, as well as the host, are labeled, rules can be created to allow or reject access across instances.

When using sVirt, the process works properly in the background, invisible to the instances themselves. Each instance's processes are labeled with a dynamically created label (500,000 are available) and these labels should extend to the actual disk images that belong to the instance's qemu-kvm process. Administrators are responsible for labeling the disk images. Once labeled, the instance no longer has any resources on the hypervisor that do not contain the label and the instance will always start with this same label.

With SELinux set to enforcing on a system with a hypervisor, basic security is automatically extended to the instance to protect the host OS from the instance process; however, without an administrator adding the system_u:object_r :virt_image_t label to the images directory and the correct labels from the process to the individual instance image files, protection will be incomplete.

Not all filesystems are compatible with SELinux labeling. For example, Ceph and not all NFS filesystems are not compatible.

SELinux and sVirt in action

The following instructions will allow you to check if SELinux is enforcing (active and protecting). Since in your lab you're running CentOS 7, you should have SELinux installed and enforcing as well as all of the installed software to make sVirt work. We will show you how to set permissions on image files in order to protect your instances:

1. Execute the following commands as root on the lab server:

 Normally, in an HA environment, you would execute this command on a compute node.

```
# getenforce
Enforcing
```

Verify that the command responds with Enforcing.

2. If, for some reason, it is any other answer, do the following and repeat the preceding command:

```
# setenforce 1
```

3. Now, check your id and your context:

```
# id
uid=0(root) gid=0(root) groups=0(root)
context=unconfined_u:unconfined_r:unconfined_t:s0-
s0:c0.c1023
```

4. Now, let's find the context for the instance running on the lab server:

 You should have at least one instance running, if you have more than one, pick the first one. If you don't have any instances running, create an instance and repeat the command.

```
# ps axZ | grep qemu-kvm

system_u:system_r:svirt_tcg_t:s0:c55,c122 7480 ?
R1     0:10 /usr/libexec/qemu-kv -name instance-
00000001
-S -machine pc-i440fx-rhel7.0.0,accel=tcg,usb=off
-m 512 -realtime mlock=off -smp
1,sockets=1,cores=1,threads=1 -uuid b803b3ce-1570-
```

```
4092-8765-4a9f76793842 -smbios
type=1,manufacturer=Fedora
Project,product=OpenStack Nova,version=13.1.0-
1.el7,serial=8184f926-0263-4305-8d8d-
d50c1472697e,uuid=b803b3ce-1570-4092-8765-
4a9f76793842,family=Virtual Machine -no-user-
config -nodefaults -chardev
socket,id=charmonitor,path=/var/lib/libvirt/
qemu/domain-instance-00000001/monitor.sock,
server,nowait -mon
chardev=charmonitor,id=monitor,mode=control -rtc
base=utc -no-shutdown -boot strict=on -device
piix3-usb-uhci,id=usb,bus=pci.0,addr=0x1.0x2 -
drive file=/var/lib/nova/instances/b803b3ce-1570-
4092-8765-4a9f76793842/disk,if=none,id=drive-
virtio-disk0,format=qcow2,cache=none -device
virtio-blk-pci,scsi=off,bus=pci.0,addr=0x4,
drive=drive-virtio-disk0,id=virtio-disk0,
bootindex=1 -netdev tap,fd=26,id=hostnet0 -device
virtio-net-pci,netdev=hostnet0,id=net0,
mac=fa:16:3e:43:48:ad,bus=pci.0,addr=0x3 -chardev
file,id=charserial0,path=/var/lib/
nova/instances/b803b3ce-1570-4092-8765-
4a9f76793842/console.log -device isa-
serial,chardev=charserial0,id=serial0 -chardev
pty,id=charserial1 -device isa-
serial,chardev=charserial1,
id=serial1 -device usb-tablet,id=input0 -vnc
0.0.0.0:0 -k en-us -vga cirrus -device
virtio-balloon-pci,id=balloon0,bus=pci.0,addr=0x5
-msg timestamp=on
```

As you can see, the first line will give the context of qemu-kvm (instance process). The instance-00000001 instance has an MCS context of system_u:system_r:svirt_tcg_t:s0:c55,c122.

5. Now, looking at the files associated with this instance in /var/lib/nova/instances/b803b3ce-1570-4092-8765-4a9f76793842/ confirms that sVirt has properly labeled them same as the instance processes (s0:c55,c122):

```
# ls -alZ /var/lib/nova/instances/b803b3ce-1570-
4092-8765-4a9f76793842/

drwxr-xr-x. nova nova
system_u:object_r:nova_var_lib_t:s0 .
```

```
drwxr-xr-x. nova nova
system_u:object_r:nova_var_lib_t:s0 ..
-rw-rw----. qemu qemu
system_u:object_r:svirt_image_t:s0:c55,c122
console.log
-rw-r--r--. qemu qemu
system_u:object_r:svirt_image_t:s0:c55,c122 disk
-rw-r--r--. nova nova
system_u:object_r:nova_var_lib_t:s0 disk.info
-rw-r--r--. nova nova
system_u:object_r:nova_var_lib_t:s0 libvirt.xml
```

If a virtual machine would happen to break out of sVirt confinement and was able to access objects on your lab server, it would only be able to use files in the same MCS context, which, in this case, is simply the image and console log, two files that are not extremely useful for compromising the host system.

 If for some reason, SELinux is set to the "Permissive" or "Disabled" mode, all of this security is disabled. Ensure SELinux remains "Enforcing" in order to receive protection from sVirt.

Since "the cloud" has become such a hot topic, cloud security has also been a very active topic lately. Keeping virtualized guests out of the host systems and out of each other's critical files is a crucial step in minimizing hypervisor break-outs. Keeping virtualized hosts isolated to their own environments allows administrators to focus on hardening the host operating systems as well as enforcing security standards for guests instead of worrying about security breaches from their own workloads. This is another reason to keep the security "zones" for OpenStack management and instances separated. Limiting access to the OpenStack management zone is essential and most enterprises setup this zone as a non-routed network, not accessible from any external networks directly.

SSL and certificate management

Devices talking to one another securely without the possibility of data compromise is a constant goal for the security community. Considering some of the recent security discoveries such as Heartbleed, BEAST, and CRIME, as well as the slew of new attacks discovered against government agencies, the need for cryptographic communications that can defeat eavesdropping attacks has increased exponentially.

In the beginning of this chapter, we defined security zones. These zones of networks and resources, along with a proper physical or logical network architecture, provide essential network and resource isolation of the different zones of an OpenStack cloud. For example, zones can be isolated with physical LAN or VLAN separation.

Assessing risk

With this best practice in mind, an administrator will first need to decide where the threat vectors are in their organization and where they are most vulnerable. One example would be the clouds that have public security zone services such as Horizon open to the Internet. Since these endpoints are exposed to networks and users that are outside the organization's control, this endpoint is an obvious choice for high-security measures. However, securing the public endpoints may not be the only encryption needed on OpenStack endpoints. Depending on the organization's network architecture, threats could come from internal networks that may be connected to more secure OpenStack zones (management or private zones). As a result, it is insufficient to simply rely on OpenStack's default security zone separation in developing encryption security policy. While adding encryption everywhere would certainly add an additional protection to all traffic, simply adding SSL/TLS encryption will provide no protection if an endpoint host is compromised. Therefore, endpoint encryption should simply be a part of a larger network and host-based security strategy.

Best practices for endpoint security

In today's standard OpenStack deployments, the default traffic over the public network is secured with SSL. While this is a good first step, best security practices dictate that all internal traffic should be treated with the same secure practices. Furthermore, due to recent SSL vulnerabilities, SSL/TLS is the only recommended encryption method unless an organization absolutely needs legacy compatibility.

TLS secures endpoints with the **Public Key Infrastructure** (**PKI**) framework. This framework is a set of processes that ensure messages are being sent securely based on verification of the identities of parties involved. PKI involves private and public keys that work in unison in order to create secure connections. These keys are certified by a **Certification Authority** (**CA**) and most companies issue their own for internal certificates. Public facing endpoints must use well known public certificate authorities in order to have the connections recognized as secure by most browsers. Therefore, with these certificates being stored in the individual hosts, host security is paramount in order to protect the private key files. If the private keys are compromised, then the security of any traffic using that key is also compromised.

Within the OpenStack ecosystem, support for TLS currently exists through libraries implemented using OpenSSL. We recommend using only TLS 1.2 as 1.1 and 1.0 are vulnerable to attack. SSL (v1-v3.0) should be avoided altogether due to many different public vulnerabilities (Heartbleed, POODLE, and so on). Most implementations today are actually TLS since TLS is the evolution of SSL. Many people call TLS 1.0 as SSL 3.1, but it is common to see the newest HTTPS implementations called either SSL/TLS or TLS/SSL. We will be using the former in this document.

It is recommended that all API endpoints in all zones be configured to use SSL/TLS. However, in certain circumstances performance can be impacted due to the processing needed to do the encryption. In use cases of high traffic, the encryption does use a significant amount of resources. In these cases, we recommend using hardware accelerators as possible options in order to offload the encryption from the hosts themselves.

The most common use case to use SSL/TLS for OpenStack endpoints is using a SSL/TLS proxy that can establish and terminate SSL/TLS sessions. While there are multiple options for this, such as Pound, Stud, nginx, HAproxy, or Apache httpd, it will be up to the administrator to choose the tool they would like to use.

Examples

The following examples will show how to install SSH/TLS for services endpoints using Apache wsgi proxy configuration for Horizon and configuring native TLS support in Keystone. These examples assume that the administrator has already secured certificates from an internal CA source. If you will be publically offering Horizon or Keystone, it is important to secure certificates from a global CA. These certificates should be recognized by all browsers and have the ability to be validated across the Internet.

Let's start with Keystone:

Now that we have our certificates, let's put them in the right place and give them adequate permissions:

```
# chown keystone /etc/pki/tls/certs/keystone.crt
# chown keystone /etc/pki/tls/private/keystone.key
```

Now we can start the serious security work. We start by adding a new SSL endpoint for Keystone and then delete the old one. First, find your current endpoints:

```
# keystone endpoint-list|grep 5000
```

Now create new ones:

```
# keystone endpoint-create --publicurl
https://openstack.example.com:5000/v2.0 --internalurl
https://openstack.example.com:5000/v2.0 --adminurl
https://openstack.example.com:35357/v2.0 --service keystone
```

Then delete the old one:

```
# keystone endpoint-delete <endpoint-id-from-above-
endpoint>
```

Edit your /etc/keystone/keystone.conf file to contain these lines:

```
[ssl]
enable = True
certfile = /etc/pki/tls/certs/keystone.crt
keyfile = /etc/pki/tls/private/keystone.key
```

Now restart the Keystone service and ensure there are no errors:

```
# service openstack-keystone restart
```

Change your environment variables in your keystonerc_admin or any other project environment files to contain the new endpoint by changing OS_AUTH_URL to:

```
OS_AUTH_URL=https://openstack.example.com:35357/v2.0/
#source keystonerc_<user>
export OS_CACERT=/path/to/certificates
```

Give it a quick test:

```
keystone endpoint-list
```

Assuming the command didn't display any errors, you can now configure the rest of your OpenStack services to connect to Keystone using SSL/TLS. The configurations are all very similar. Here is an example of Nova. You will need to edit the `/etc/nova/nova.conf` file to look like this:

```
[keystone_authtoken]
auth_protocol = https
auth_port = 35357
auth_host = openstack.example.com
auth_uri = https://openstack.example.com:5000/v2.0
cafile = /path/to/ca.crt
```

Cinder, Glance, Neutron, Swift, Ceilometer, and so on are all the same. Here is a list of configuration files you will need to edit:

- `/etc/openstack-dashboard/local_settings` (Horizon access to Keystone)
- `/etc/ceilometer/ceilometer.conf`
- `/etc/glance/glance-api.conf`
- `/etc/neutron/neutron.conf`
- `/etc/neutron/api-paste.ini`
- `/etc/neutron/metadata_agent.ini`
- `/etc/glance/glance-registry.conf`
- `/etc/cinder/cinder.conf`
- `/etc/cinder/api-paste.ini`
- `/etc/swift/proxy-server.conf`

Once these or any other service configuration files have been modified, restart all of your services and test your cloud:

```
# openstack-service restart
# service httpd restart
# openstack-status
```

You should see all of your services running and online. You have now encrypted traffic between your OpenStack services and Keystone, a very important step in keeping your cloud secure. If not, check your services log files for errors.

Now we configure Horizon to encrypt connections to clients using SSL/TLS.

On the controller node, add the following (or modify the existing configuration to match) in `/etc/apache2/apache2.conf` on Ubuntu and `/etc/httpd/conf/httpd.conf` on RHEL:

```
<VirtualHost <ip address>:80>
  ServerName <site FQDN>
  RedirectPermanent / https://<site FQDN>/
</VirtualHost>
<VirtualHost <ip address>:443>
  ServerName <site FQDN>
  SSLEngine On
  SSLProtocol +TLSv1 +TLSv1.1 +TLSv1.2,
  SSLCipherSuite
  HIGH:!RC4:!MD5:!aNULL:!eNULL:!EXP:!LOW:!MEDIUM
  SSLCertificateFile    /path/<site FQDN>.crt
  SSLCACertificateFile  /path/<site FQDN>.crt
  SSLCertificateKeyFile /path/<site FQDN>.key
  WSGIScriptAlias / <WSGI script location>
  WSGIDaemonProcess horizon user=<user> group=<group>
  processes=3 threads=10
  Alias /static <static files location>
  <Directory <WSGI dir>>
    # For http server 2.2 and earlier:
    Order allow,deny
    Allow from all

    # Or, in Apache http server 2.4 and later:
    # Require all granted
  </Directory>
</VirtualHost>
```

On the compute servers, the default configuration of the `libvirt` daemon is to not allow remote access. However, live migrating an instance between OpenStack compute nodes requires remote `libvirt` daemon access between the compute nodes. Obviously, unauthenticated remote access is not allowable in most cases; therefore, we can setup `libvirtd` TCP socket with SSL/TLS for the encryption and X.509 client certificates for authentication.

In order to allow remote access to `libvirtd` (assuming you are using the KVM hypervisor), you will need to adjust some `libvertd` configuration directives. By default, these directives are commented out but will need to be adjusted to the following in `etc/libvirt/libvirtd.conf`:

```
listen_tls = 1
listen_tcp = 0
auth_tls = "none"
```

When setting the `auth_tls` directive to `"none"`, the `libvirt` daemon is expecting X.509 certificates for authentication. Also, when using SSL/TLS, a nondefault URI is required for live migration. This will need to be set in `/etc/nova/nova.conf`:

```
live_migration_uri=qemu+tls://%s/system
```

For more information on generating certificates for libvirt, refer to the libvirt documentation at `http://libvirt.org/remote.html#Remote_certificates`.

It is also important to take other security measures for protecting libvirt, such as restricting network access to your compute nodes to only other compute nodes on access ports for TLS. Also, by default, the `libvirt` daemon listens for connections on all interfaces. This should be restricted by editing the `listen_addr` directive in `/etc/libvirt/libvirtd.conf`:

```
listen_addr = <IP address or hostname>
```

Additionally, live-migration uses a large amount of random ports to do live migrations. However, after the initial request is established via SSL/TLS on the daemon port, these random ports do not continue to use SSL/TLS. However, it is possible to tunnel this additional traffic over the regular `libvirtd` daemon port. This is accomplished by modifying some additional directives in the `/etc/nova/nova.conf` configuration file:

```
live_migration_flag=VIR_MIGRATE_UNDEFINE_SOURCE,
VIR_MIGRATE_PEER2PEER, VIR_MIGRATE_TUNNELLED
```

> The tunneling of migration traffic across the libvirt daemon port does not apply to block migration. Block migration is still only available by random ports.

Auditing OpenStack

As more enterprises are bringing production workloads to OpenStack, the need for audit compliance increases exponentially. These same enterprises may have specialized audit requirements for compliance with PCI, FEDRAMP, SOX, and HIPPA and without a way to audit what is happening in their cloud they are out of compliance. These enterprises are used to having this capability in legacy platforms, therefore, it only makes sense that they should require it with OpenStack.

This auditing needs to be done in a manner that the enterprises are accustomed to, and they should not be expected to have to ingest different log formats from each of the core OpenStack projects in a disparate fashion as they sometimes have to do today. However, the good news is, there is one format that provides a normalized and federated way to collect and analyze audit data. This format is the **Cloud Auditing Data Federation** (**CADF**) standard. The CADF standard defines a full event model anyone can use to fill in the essential data needed to certify, self-manage, and self-audit application security in cloud environments. This functionality is needed to build trust for the cloud platform and increase adoption. Enterprises need to feel that they are able to track and detect unauthorized access on their cloud platform.

CADF details

According to the Distributed Management Task Force, the governing body of CADF, the CADF standard does the following:

> *"defines a normative event data model along with a compatible set of interfaces for federating events, logs and reports between cloud providers and customers. CADF provides several benefits to customers of cloud services. Audit event data can be represented in a common format to allow for consistent reporting of this data across different cloud providers. Cloud customers will also be able to aggregate data from different cloud providers to provide a more complete and consistent picture of all audit data. Also with audit data coming in from different providers in the same format, customers will be able to use common audit tools and processes for all their audit data. The ability to federate data from different sources will also provide benefits to users of OpenStack with an audit data format that will be consistent across a collection of disparate cloud (IaaS) services with some common components such as Keystone and Oslo libraries. These components will need to share audit data."*

The CADF specification contains an event model that specifies taxonomies for any event that can be audited, these are as follows:

- **Resource**: The classification of the event by logical resource that is related to the event. Basically, this is who was the intended target or what observed the event.
- **Action**: This is used to classify what action caused the event.
- **Outcome**: This describes what the outcome of the action was.

Furthermore, there are mandatory properties of the preceding taxonomies, these further break down the event into the following five components:

Model Component	CADF Definition
OBSERVER	The RESOURCE that generates the CADF Event Record based on its observation (directly or indirectly) of the Actual Event.
INITIATOR	The RESOURCE that initiated, originated, or instigated the event's ACTION, according to the OBSERVER.
ACTION	The operation or activity the INITIATOR has performed, attempted to perform or has pending against the event's TARGET, according to the OBSERVER.
TARGET	The RESOURCE against which the ACTION of a CADF Event Record was performed, was attempted, or is pending, according to the OBSERVER. Note: a TARGET (in the CADF Event Model) can represent a plurality of target resources.
OUTCOME	The result or status of the ACTION against the TARGET, according to the OBSERVER.

Required CADF event model components – CADF-OpenStack

Using these properties, the CADF data model is designed to provide the "who", "what", "when", "where", "from where", and "where to" of an activity. Most people in security have heard of the 5 W's of audit and compliance, however, this model was designed for cloud environments and adds an additional two (from where and where to).

In order to further explain how CADF is used in audit, based on the 7 W's, refer to the following chart:

"W" Component	CADF Mandatory Properties	CADF Optional Properties (where applicable)	Description
What	event.action event.outcome event.type	event.reason *(e.g., severity, reason code, policy id)*	"what" activity occurred; "what" was the result
When	event.eventTime	reporter.timestamp (detailed), *for each reporter* event.duration	"when" did it happen • Any granularity via ISO 8601 format
Who	initiator.id initiator.type	initiator.id (id, name): (basic) initiator.credential (token): (detailed) initiator.credential.assertions (precise)	"who" (person or service) initiated the action
FromWhere		initiator.addresses (basic) initiator.host (agents, platforms, ...) (detailed) Initiator.geolocation (precise)	FromWhere provides information describ ing where the action was initiated from. May include • logical/physical addresses • ISO-6709-2008, precise geolocations
OnWhat	target.id target.type		"onWhat" resource did the activity target
Where	observer.id observer.type	reporterstep.role (detailed) reporterstep.reporterTime (detailed)	"where" did the activity get observed (reported), or modified in some way.
ToWhere		target.addresses (basic) target.host (agents, platforms, ...) (detailed) target.geolocation (precise)	ToWhere provides information describing where the target resource that is affected by the action is located. For example, this can be as simple as an IP address or server name.

CADF – the 7 W's of audit – CADF OpenStack

Using CADF with OpenStack

Except for a few special cases, getting CADF information out of OpenStack services is pretty straightforward. However, depending on the distribution, these instructions may differ. The following instructions show how Nova can be enabled for CADF audit events to be sent to Ceilometer (optionally log files). This is done via the Keystone middleware, which provides an optional WSGI middleware filter which allows the ability to audit API requests for each component of OpenStack.

First, log in to your OpenStack deployment. Edit the `/etc/nova/api-paste.ini` file. At the end of the file, add the following:

```
[filter:audit]
paste.filter_factory = pycadf.middleware.audit:AuditMiddleware.factory
audit_map_file = /etc/nova/api_audit_map.conf
```

Review the `[composite:openstack_compute_api_v2]` settings and verify that the values match the following sample:

```
[composite:openstack_compute_api_v2]
use = call:nova.api.auth:pipeline_factory
noauth = faultwrap sizelimit noauth ratelimit
osapi_compute_app_v2
keystone = faultwrap sizelimit authtoken
keystonecontext ratelimit audit osapi_compute_app_v2
keystone_nolimit = faultwrap sizelimit authtoken
keystonecontext audit osapi_compute_app_v2
```

Additional options are available to redirect the events to log files as well as messaging. Simply add the following:

```
[audit_middleware_notifications]
driver = log
```

Now, copy the `api_audit_map.conf` file to the `/etc/nova/` directory and restart the API service.

The command to restart the API service is OS-specific. On Redhat Enterprise Linux systems, the command is `service openstack-nova-api restart`. To know more, refer to `https ://access.redhat.com/documentation/en-US/Red_Hat_Enterprise_Linux_OpenStack_ Platform/2/html/Getting_Started_Guide/chap-Deploying_Compute_Services.html`

Open the `entry_points.txt` file in the `egg-info` subdirectory of your OpenStack installation directory.

For PackStack installations, the file path looks similar to `/usr/lib/python2.7/site-packages/ceilometer-2014.2-py2.7.egg-info/entry_points.txt`.

While this example was only for Nova, there are preconfigured `api_audit_map.conf` files for other services such as Glance, Ceilometer, Cinder, Neutron, and so on at `https://github.com/openstack/pycadf/tree/master/etc/pycadf`. By following the preceding steps and using these `api_audit_map.conf` files, you can enable all core OpenStack services for CADF eventing.

Since the events are stored to messaging, and events, by default are sent to Ceilometer, this is where you will find your events stored. In order to query Ceilometer for Keystone events, you should first execute a Keystone action that would cause an event, for example:

```
$ openstack user create test_user --os-identity-api-
version 3 --os-auth-url http://10.0.2.15:5000/v3 --os-
default-domain default
```

In order to get the event that this created out of Ceilometer, you should do the following:

```
$ ceilometer event-list --query
event_type=identity.user.created
```

Which will result in the following type of output:

```
+------------------------+-------------------------------------------------+
| Event Type             | Traits                                          |
+------------------------+-------------------------------------------------+
| identity.user.created  | +----------------+----------+------------------  |
|                        | |     name       |   type   |    value          |
|                        | +----------------+----------+------------------  |
|                        | | initiator_id   | string   | asd123j123312yf34212339e6e424a7f |
|                        | | project_id     | string   | ae7e3k14k202042j22f19bc25c8c09f0 |
|                        | | resource_id    | string   | 22a21766c478927349e3fda7ee0b712b |
|                        | |   service      | string   | identity.openstack.example.com   |
|                        | +----------------+----------+------------------  |
```

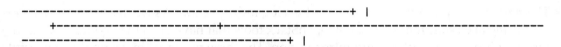

As we can see in the preceding output, we have an audit trail of who created the user from the preceding command as well as what the project was and the resource ID. This data and all of the data from the other services combined would provide a 7 W's audit trail for this user's transactions as well as any other transactions in this cloud. Using either open source tools such as Ansible, Puppet, or Chef to create query automation for Ceilometer, log files or having Ceilometer feed this event data to something like IBM's QRadar `http://www-03.ibm.com/software/products/en/qradar` which is, according to IBM:

> *"[A] security intelligence platform that combines traditional **security information and event management (SIEM)** and log management capabilities with **network behavior anomaly detection(NBAD)**, vulnerability assessment and management, risk analysis and simulation and forensic data inspection. It consumes events, flows, asset and vulnerability information and network topology by integrating with other products/applications/services/assets/endpoints in a client's environment (on-premises or in the cloud), enabling users to view, analyze, understand and report on everything going on in their environment from many different angles and perspectives."*

QRadar integrates with OpenStack as a consumer of Ceilometer data. It then takes the CADF formatted data in the platform to do the analysis.

Log aggregation and analysis

As we saw in the previous section, we have an audit trail of who created the user from the demonstrated command as well as what the project was and the resource ID. This data and all of the data from the other services combined will provide a 7 W's audit trail for this user's transactions as well as any other transactions in this cloud. However, since we now have audit data, we can start looking for security attacks. Some of these attacks may be as follows:

- Real-time security alerts for brute force attacks OpenStack
- Detecting malicious or unauthorized access to virtual machines, volumes, or images
- Accidental or intentional cloud service outages
- Compliance reporting for all user activity in OpenStack

These types of attacks can all be detected via log introspection. As we discussed in Chapter 5, *Building to Operate* there is a set of OpenStack tools that have been the de-facto standard for log shipping, formatting, and introspection. The three tools that make up this powerful combination are Elasticsearch (the searching module), Logstash (the log shipping tool), and Kibana (the visualization engine and dashboard). While we discussed these tools mostly in an operational viewpoint in Chapter 5, *Building to Operate* these same tools can be used to detect, in real time, all of the attacks listed earlier. The main advantages of this stack are as follows:

- Open Source search server written in Java
- Used to index many types of heterogeneous data
- Real-time search through indexing
- REST API web interface that outputs JSON

A best architectural practice in this area would be to use LogStash in a distributed fashion to centralize all log files with CADF data to a secure host running ElasticSearch and Kibana. LogStash would then be configured to index the highly normalized CADF logs and limits would be created to alert on threshold breaches.

For example, if the CADF logs detected thousands of failed Keystone authentication events from the same IP address within a short time period. Chances are, this is a brute force attack and warrants an alert to the security and network teams.

Using Kibana, the teams can search through the audit logs and determine how long the attacks have been occurring, if anyone valid is logging in through the same subnet, or any number of other analytics.

There are quite a few other SIEM platforms that do OpenStack integrations and can ingest either log files or Ceilometer feeds, some are listed here:

- Symantec Security Information Manager
- Splunk
- HP/Arcsight
- Tripwire
- NetIQ
- Quest Software
- Enterprise Security Manager

While both the open source and commercial solutions have great sets of features, it is up to each individual enterprise to evaluate SIEM solutions. However, with the preceding information, an administrator can feel empowered to enable CADF event logging for OpenStack and provide any platform with the data it needs to satisfy corporate audit requirements.

Summary

In this chapter, you learned some holistic approaches to OpenStack security. This includes not only the applications running on top of OpenStack but the projects that make up the platform as well as the underlying operating environments. You learned that enterprise OpenStack security is not only encryption, logging, or patching but a much more enterprise-based approach in which all solutions must work in harmony with others. Sometimes this interoperability can be achieved with configurations, other times it calls for additional open source or commercial grade enterprise software depending on security requirements. However, a very important point is to realize that OpenStack is no more insecure than its competing platforms and that there are strategies and tools available to make OpenStack compliant with most enterprise security policies.

References

- https://security.openstack.org/ossalist.html
- https://review.openstack.org/#/c/299025/
- https://wiki.openstack.org/wiki/Vulnerability_Management
- https://www.openstack.org/assets/survey/April-2016-User-Survey-Report.pdf)
- http://www.pulpproject.org/
- http://libvirt.org/remote.html#Remote_certificates
- http://www-03.ibm.com/software/products/en/qradar
- https://github.com/openstack/pycadf/tree/master/etc/pycadf

8
Conclusion

In the year and a half since we started writing this book, OpenStack has changed enough that we've had to rewrite most of the code examples at least once. Our hope is that the approach we've outlined in the previous chapters will help Cloud Architects develop and deploy private clouds using OpenStack in spite of the rapid rate of change in the software ecosystem. In this last chapter, we'll talk about some of the emerging trends in OpenStack and how to build a road map for your organization for its adoption of Infrastructure as a Service.

Emerging trends in OpenStack

One of the most interesting things about the way that OpenStack has evolved over its short history is the vast number of projects that have sprung up around the core set of compute, network, and storage services. As of the Newton release of OpenStack, there were almost sixty projects in the "Big Tent". These projects can be broadly lumped into two categories – those which automate additional infrastructure components and those which manage the installation, configuration, and life cycle of OpenStack itself. This first set of projects are typically patterned after analogues in Amazon Web Services and provide a fuller "stack" of services to be used in application deployments. The second set of projects contain configuration management code such as the Puppet modules we used in earlier chapters to deploy OpenStack and common services and libraries that are used by the other services.

Moving up the stack

Some of the projects that automate additional infrastructure components have become adopted widely enough to be included with commercial vendors' OpenStack distributions. These include projects such as Trove, which provides Database as a Service, and Sahara, which provides Data Processing as a Service. These projects leverage the Nova compute service to deploy instances of prepared Glance images that provide end users with higher-level resources such as databases over the OpenStack APIs. These resources can then be automated like any other OpenStack resource either via the API or via the Heat orchestration service.

Trove is one of the more mature OpenStack services outside of the core set of original services. Trove allows developers to provision an instance of a given database to support their application without having to design or specify the underlying compute and storage for the database instance. Trove is largely developed by the company Tesora, who offers a certified and supported version of the Trove component for most of the major community and enterprise distributions of OpenStack. At present, Trove supports provisioning a range of relational databases such as MySQL and Oracle in addition to NoSQL databases such as MongoDB and Redis.

Sahara provides Big Data as a Service in OpenStack, largely through the automated deployment of Hadoop clusters. Sahara allows users to create a data processing cluster, define job templates, and then execute those jobs on the cluster. Sahara has a large number of integration points to external services, such as Designate for name resolution and Barbican for certificate management. Jobs can pull data either from external or internal HDFS volumes or from Swift or Manila in OpenStack. Sahara currently supports Apache Hadoop, the Hortonworks Data Platform, Apache Spark, MapR, and Cloudera Hadoop as cluster types. Both traditional Hadoop and Spark jobs are supported in the service.

Designate and Barbican are examples of services that provide extended infrastructure automation capabilities to round out application stacks, but do not provision instances. Another popular project in this category is Zaqar, which provides Messaging as a Service. Services like these can be extremely attractive to both developers and operators in private cloud environments. Developers no longer have to worry about the details behind the infrastructure components in their application architecture and operators can rest assured that developers are using these components in standardized ways that are easy to troubleshoot and scale.

The impact of containers

Linux containers have taken the technology world by storm in the last few years and they have impacted OpenStack in two different areas. First of all, OpenStack is now seen as one of the most flexible infrastructures for the deployment of container-based Platform as a Service technologies such as Kubernetes and Cloud Foundry. Secondly, OpenStack is now increasingly deployed as a set of containerized services. Additional Big Tent projects have sprung up around both of these use cases for containers in OpenStack.

Magnum is a popular project that automates the provisioning of container orchestration environments. Magnum uses the Nova compute service to provision these environments inside of OpenStack tenants in the same way that Trove and Sahara do. As of the Newton release of OpenStack, Magnum supports Docker Swarm, Kubernetes, and Apache Mesos clusters, abstracted as "bays" for containers. Another popular project focused on containers is Kuryr, which allows users to bridge Neutron networks from the infrastructure layer into the application layer.

Perhaps the largest emerging change in the management and deployment of OpenStack is the use of containers to deploy OpenStack services. This work was pioneered in the Kolla project, which uses Ansible and Docker to deploy and manage OpenStack services. It has since spread to other projects – the Fuel installer is currently moving to a Docker-based deployment strategy and the OpenStack-Ansible project (OSA) uses LXC containers to deploy OpenStack services. As these efforts gain consensus, organizations should evaluate whether or not a container-based deployment methodology works well for them.

Building the roadmap

It's an exciting time to be involved in such a rapidly changing project. That excitement should be leveraged by a Cloud Architect who is looking to gain adoption from application development teams. One way to build interest in the developer community is to continually expand the amount of services that are available to them in the private cloud. As we mentioned earlier, adding capabilities from services such as Trove or Designate to the cloud simplifies the work that both developers and operators do. Including developer teams as early-adopters of new features is a great way to build rapport and confidence with them as well.

Introducing new features

A prerequisite for being able to incrementally add new features to an OpenStack deployment is to have a set of test environments available to advance the features through. Cloud engineering teams should have a private environment where they can develop and test new features and another environment where end users can test features before they are rolled out to production cloud environments. Having multiple environments also allows new functionality to bake in, which allows cloud operators the ability to see what the logging, performance, and other impacts of a new feature will be. Instrumentation can also be developed and tested in the lower environments.

New features or capabilities should be introduced incrementally into the platform. In the planning stage, use cases for the capabilities should be defined and test cases should be written. These new features and capabilities should also be tested and deployed in the same manner as code; first in test environments, then into production. As the features are deployed into lower environments, documentation should be updated and test cases for the capabilities should be added to the monitoring regimen. A simple way to test these new capabilities is to write an example Heat orchestration template that exercises them. For example, adding the provisioning of a database to an existing application stack that is already being deployed by Heat. This template can then also be provided to application teams as documentation for the service.

Releasing new versions

One of the most discussed and criticised aspects of OpenStack has always been the major version upgrade procedure. On the upside though, it's also one of the most thoroughly documented and tested aspects of the project. Each major component of OpenStack provides an upgrade path between releases and most of them support rolling upgrades at this point. Much work has been done to de couple the API versions of the various services to ensure that services can be updated one at a time without downtime. The truth is, though, that it's hard to upgrade an operating private cloud. Users of private clouds expect their workloads to be continuously available. As such, many of the OpenStack adopters that we've worked with have been reluctant to update their clouds once they're in production.

While deploying a release of OpenStack and then running it for a few years is certainly possible (commercial vendors such as Red Hat provide support for up to three years for a given release of OpenStack), we certainly don't recommend it. Organizations who deployed the Icehouse release of OpenStack and have run it for a couple of years will end up re-engineering much of their configuration management and deployment processes for the Newton release. This work takes a lot of time and effort. Organizations who have stepped through the releases or have deployed a new release every calendar year will have a much smaller amount of change to manage when the new version does come out.

Incremental change has a smaller impact on the developer community as well. As we mentioned previously, continually improving and updating your Infrastructure as a Service will keep the community engaged and eliminate the need to retrain them every time a new platform is released.

Summary

In this book, we've walked through the major areas of focus in the emerging practice of a Cloud Architect as it pertains to OpenStack. We've shown you some techniques and recommendations to enable you to work with company stakeholders and provide architectural leadership in order to create a holistic design for OpenStack in an enterprise. Successfully designing, deploying, and operating OpenStack clouds requires a wide breadth of knowledge in the fields of compute, network, storage, and software design. It also takes a deep understanding of a company's strategic mission, processes, and success criteria for implementing a private cloud. Successful Cloud Architects leverage the knowledge and practice of subject matter experts in deep technical areas in conjunction with their own knowledge when designing OpenStack clouds. This book was written to provide a framework that an Architect could use to create a successful OpenStack deployment in concert with the rest of an enterprise using modern software development methodologies. While this book provides a solid foundation for OpenStack architecture, we hope it has given you the tools and confidence to begin your own journey into OpenStack architectural design.

References

OpenStack projects – `http://governance.openstack.org/reference/projects/`

Index

www.ingramcontent.com/pod-product-compliance
Lightning Source LLC
Chambersburg PA
CBHW060557060326
40690CB00017B/3735